A SURROGATE FOR HEAVEN

BREAKING THE SILENCE ABOUT MISCARRIAGE

NICOLE HAHN

authorHOUSE®

AuthorHouse™
1663 Liberty Drive
Bloomington, IN 47403
www.authorhouse.com
Phone: 1 (800) 839-8640

Published by AuthorHouse 12/15/2016

ISBN: 978-1-5246-5392-7 (sc)
ISBN: 978-1-5246-5391-0 (e)

DEDICATION

To my angels who left our Earthly world for a better place. I never got to meet you, my best friends, but you will always be a piece of me and live in my heart. I'll never forget you. I promise to treasure all of life's blessings in your honor.

ACKNOWLEDGEMENTS

My sincerest thanks go out to each heartbroken or grieving parent who has given me the opportunity to visit such a private part of their heart through this book. Thank you to anyone who picked up this book or clicked it open on your ereader with an open mind and let me discuss something very personal. Thank you to my husband for showing me so much love, especially on days when I'm tough to love and for feeling comfortable enough and giving me the okay to share our story with the world. To my dear parents, thank you for always encouraging me to make goals and fight for them. Above all else, I thank God for gracing me with the ability to help others through my experiences.

Contents

1

BUT FIRST, A FEW COMMENTS

We all have something we're afraid to share; a sliver of truth that we think will make us appear weak in the eyes of society. It takes a rare form of courage to share or open up about something so personal. I read the other day that the two most powerful words in the English language are "me too." When you expose those vulnerable areas, more often than not, you discover that you're not alone in your struggles. You're mad, sad, distraught, or lost? There are plenty of others out there who can answer, "me too." Even people you look up to confront challenges just like you.

Culture bullies us into not sharing our stories about pregnancy loss. Few of us have the fortitude to combat that force. When I first started writing this book and friends or family would ask what it is about, I would be a little hesitant in how I would answer. I didn't write a romance novel, mystery, or thriller. I wrote something real, fresh, and personal. I had told a few friends and family a couple of details about my husband and I's story, but until now, I hadn't bared it all.

Research for this book led me to an article about Christie Brinkley and her experiences with pregnancy loss. That article wasn't very kind. The man who wrote it criticized her for speaking out about her miscarriages, saying that her private life should stay just that - private. Individuals like the man who wrote that article are partially to blame for why the majority of women are too afraid to talk about their losses, making it difficult to find a safe place that provides support. Letting people, some being strangers, into that part of your heart is a bit daunting, but I'm telling my story. I'm not afraid of judgment or criticism. I'm not ashamed of my story. Being quiet about pregnancy loss needs to end and I want to help us get there. Silence breeds silence, so we need to stop being so dang quiet. I knew nothing about miscarriage until it happened to me. Although nothing can prepare you and you'll never be able to fully comprehend what it's like until you experience it, we can all do a better job of initiating that discussion.

I don't expect you to care about how everything in this book has affected me personally. I want to share my story so that you know you're not alone. You're not crazy, a horrible person, or unreasonable for feeling the way you do. I believe a great way to help ourselves heal is by helping to heal others. If I can help one person, this book will be a success. When I suffered through miscarriages, I desperately sought people to relate to and I hunted for stories that somewhat mirrored my own in one way or another, just to know that I wasn't the only one. I always felt a sense of aloneness in that fact that none of my friends could relate to what I was going through. From what I knew, the friends who had tried seemed to get pregnant quickly and carried babies fearlessly and without much complication, if any.

Hopefully, some of you will discover a little bit of yourselves nestled in the chapters of this book. If not, I'm glad, but instead I hope you acquire insight into a complex world that most are afraid to talk about or prefer to pretend doesn't exist. A majority of the struggles my husband and I have encountered are not unique to us. Many couples have dealt with or are dealing with pregnancy loss, but too many are afraid to speak up, like it's a dirty secret of which to be ashamed. I hope my story can disprove that and help anyone who has lost someone special.

In the first weeks after losing a baby, it certainly won't feel like it but things will get better and you're far from being alone in this mess. The misfortunes that have touched my husband and I have given us experience useful in supporting others who are rowing in the same canoe. Sharing my story is therapeutic for my own benefit, but also I want to tell you our truths so that you can find your story, whatever that may be, in my words.

When people try to cheer up or talk to women who have miscarried, they mean well. I know they do, but it doesn't always feel that way. Being a woman who has been impacted by multiple pregnancy losses gives me the ability to empathize a little bit with the hurt thoughtless comments can cause. I won't ever say that I know how you feel, because I don't know how exactly you're feeling. I can only tell you how I feel and let you know that I understand to an extent. I can relate on a certain level. I hope that after reading this book, you can navigate differently around ignorant or insensitive comments. Find a way to find your new "normal."

This book isn't intended to be an instruction manual on coping, because there is no "right" way to manage the devastation that comes from pregnancy loss. It's simply my husband and I's story and it's special to us. Despite the pain, I want to remember. I never want to forget a single thing, because I've grown as a person and developed a special connection with God in result. I want our children that I hope to have someday to read this and know exactly what their mom and dad went through trying to bring them into the world.

2

WHAT I WISH SOMEONE HAD TOLD ME

Dear woman in tears leaving the Obstetrician's office,

I don't know your name or exact circumstances, but know that you're not alone. When I saw you and your husband solemnly trudge through the waiting room with slumped shoulders and dart to the exit as if the building was on fire, red in the face with a glossy haze clouding your eyes, I knew that you received bad news. I know that look all too well, because I've been in your shoes more than once. My heart hurts for you.

I will never forget walking into that first ultrasound appointment, innocent and hopeful to see a little baby growing on the screen and hear a heartbeat. Unfortunately, we were given bad news, too. I remember mustering up the courage to walk back out into the waiting room full of happy expecting moms or mommies with their little ones, and bursting into more tears as soon as I could make it out the door. I wanted to hug you today and tell you that you're not alone, but maybe you're not ready for that and I'm a complete stranger. I didn't want to risk it.

I wanted to tell you that the days to come won't be easy. In fact, they're really going to suck and you'll question your faith, among every other possible thing there is to question. No, life isn't fair. But, months will pass and you won't cry as much. You'll never forget the baby that had to leave way too soon, but the sharp edges will dull.

You'll be angry a lot and that's okay. You may even take that anger out on the wrong people. You have every right to feel every emotion. Don't let anyone tell you to just get over it. You'll probably feel the worst when you're alone and secluded with only your own thoughts, so try your hardest to get out, enjoy the days, and be with your friends. Your skin needs some sunlight, girl! That may seem impossible, but you're stronger than you think. Doctors or nurses may treat you like what happened was a sickness you'll just get over or they might brush it aside because pregnancy loss is somewhat common, but they don't know you. Even though I don't know you either, I have a little bit of understanding of how much this hurts and I'm on your side. Maybe you'll read this and it will bring some comfort. Maybe it won't. Again, I just want you to know you're not alone.

Sincerely,
Another member of the dreaded "club"

3

A WHOLE NEW WORLD

I'm in my late twenties, pay bills, work an eight-to-five job, and yet, it still hasn't fully hit me that I'm an adult and have to face adult-like issues. Sometimes, I reminisce and long for the days when my biggest concern was whether or not the cute guy I had a crush on at school would like the color of top I was wearing. Like a lot of people, when I was younger I had my whole life outlined, and was fairly confident that things would just fall into place. Life isn't that easy and now that I think about it, I'm not sure why I was so confident back then. In any case, my plan was to find my perfect match, date for about a year, be married by twenty three, and start having babies within a year after that. Simple, right? This book is largely about how wrong I was and how God's plan is not our own.

When I was in high school, it was hammered into my head that if you have sex at a young age, you will get pregnant and die. Okay, maybe that's a bit dramatic, but the importance of practicing safe sex or waiting until you're married was stressed. At fifteen, my mother took me into the doctor to get started on birth control. Oh, no, I didn't start having sex at that age. I didn't even have my first kiss until sixteen! Primarily, my mom started buying me the pill in attempt to help with break-out problems and regulate my menstrual cycle. It was smart of her to have me begin birth control pills early, before I'd ever be put in a situation where I'd need them for their intended purpose.

From the time I started taking birth control and when I did become sexually active, the fear of becoming pregnant was instilled in me. I always had dreams of going to college, which is entirely possible if you have a child. Many young parents continue on after high school to get their degrees, but I knew having children didn't make that ambition easy. I also knew it was important to me to experience certain things in my younger years that I wouldn't be able to indulge in when I have kids. I believe it's important to have those crazy years of taking chances and making mistakes, partying in college, or simply being able to make decisions without having to factor in another human being dependent on you. At a young age, I decided that I wanted to live my life by the book, how I was always told it is "supposed to go." I wanted a home life similar to what my sweet grandparents had. I wanted to be young and crazy.

Then, I wanted to find a nice guy, settle down, and have babies – exactly like that.

For the most part, my life had gone according to plan. I lived up to my goal of enjoying my "young and crazy" college years. I met my husband playing trombone in the marching band in college together. I received my degree in four years. My Prince Charming and I fell in love and got married. God had answered my prayer when I prayed for a compassionate, patient, and loving man to share my life with. We went on a beautiful Alaskan cruise for our honeymoon, but not immediately after our wedding. My husband and I thought that around the time of our honeymoon would be perfect for me to go off of the pill and we'd start trying to start our little family. We had been together for over two years and married for about eight months by then. We were ready to add to our duo.

Everything was so exciting. God is good. How lucky was I to have been blessed with the most incredible man, have a beautiful wedding, go on our dream honeymoon, move into a large house, land a job that I never thought I'd be doing, and be truly happy for the first time in my life? My husband and I were at the ideal point in our lives to start having children and we were hopeful, confident. We both had great jobs and all of our student loan debt was paid. Not many newlyweds can say that they are completely debt free. We were ready for babies. I started paying closer attention to my friends with children, how they handled themselves and soaked up what having a child might be like.

I didn't grow up in an environment that had children. My family is fairly small. I'm an only child and have one cousin. Having only one first cousin is pretty rare. When I was younger, our family gatherings were fairly quiet the few times we saw each other each year. My family is well spread across the states from Georgia to Minnesota, so we only see each other at Christmas, for the most part. I didn't know of any friends that had kids, either. Unlike most teenage girls, I never babysat. So, being the planner that I am and realizing that I had no experience with little ones, I started Googling and surfing the web, visiting any baby website or forum I could click on, because I had a feeling that it was going to happen soon for us. Everything else in my "plan" seemed to fall into place, so why not this part too?

I immediately immersed myself in this whole new world that I had obviously never been a part of before. The experience is similar to when you're a Junior or Senior in high school and you start looking into colleges for your future. You research, send emails, make phone calls, and pay visits to campuses. Your level of excitement is sky-high and the anticipation for that next big step in your life builds. Just like college-searching, preparing yourself to become a parent consisted of lots of researching, like visiting and joining various trying-to-conceive forums. Doing so really benefitted me, as I didn't realize that there was a precise timing for everything, a process, a checklist, or certain things to do to increase your chances of becoming pregnant. Heck, I didn't know trying to have a baby would be so complicated in general. I know now that conceiving is actually a miracle, but back then I thought it would magically happen according to my plan. It's beyond frustrating to think about how I stressed and spent so much money on contraceptives over the years in attempt to not get pregnant before I was ready. Then, when the time came when my husband and I wanted to have a baby, it ended up being an arduous quest and long road no one should have to travel.

4

JUST GOOGLE IT

We live in an age where it's hard for us to think for ourselves. We're afraid of making mistakes of any kind, so the minute we need reassurance or help, we sprint with warp speed to the internet. At least for the folks my age (under thirty), Googling something is our first thought. How long should I cook the chicken for this recipe? Google it. My dog is choking on a piece of hot dog, how do I save him? Is there such a thing as the doggie Heimlich? Google it. We're going on vacation and we'll be at the beach a lot. Is spray or lotion form of sunscreen best? I better Google it, to make sure.

The downside to this obsession of finding answers on the internet is that anyone can write an article on the World Wide Web. Anyone with the competency of using a keyboard can comment or post a question in a forum or on a blog. People who aren't completely informed, or who have been incorrectly informed, have the power to put things on the internet that are false, filling we poor readers' heads with junk. I'll admit I'm very gullible. I eat all of that information right up.

On the upside, the internet gives us women who are excited, concerned, worried, or devastated about pregnancy, a vehicle to release our feelings and to support others. By sharing our experiences, asking questions, or just being involved in the online community, we are helping the world open its eyes to the widespread nature of pregnancy loss and difficulties involved with trying to become pregnant.

I quickly learned that when you start trying to have children, you're not supposed to talk about the process, your feelings, or any of it really. The personal benefit of not telling people that you're trying to conceive is less pressure. Having people ask you how it's going, why you're not pregnant yet, or "when is that baby (that doesn't exist yet) due?" when you're trying creates more stress and compounds the pressure that you already feel. When it comes to others, trying to conceive is something people just don't talk about. It's an understood rule. God forbid you make anyone feel uncomfortable with feelings and honesty. If you're lucky enough to get pregnant, you're still supposed to remain quiet until after the first trimester because of the risk of miscarriage. Frankly, I'm tired of it. I'm tired of staying quiet so that others can feel comfortable. Just like any other loss, miscarriage mamas and daddies need support too. No one should have to stay quiet or hide when we are worried, sad, or grieving.

Getting involved in the online community is a small step in the right direction of breaking the silence.

Having said that, the online community full of women and men trying to conceive can be overwhelming. When I confronted it for the first time, I could hardly understand what some of the people who were posting were talking about. In fact, I had to look up a terminology glossary. For example, we can't simply say "trying to conceive." Instead, it's shortened to "TTC." Aunt Flo becomes "AF," Basal body temperature becomes "BBT," Sex becomes "BD" (baby dance), Cervical mucus becomes "CM," Days past ovulation becomes "DPO," Luteal phase becomes "LP,"... etc. Setting aside the fact that all of those terms were being abbreviated, I barely knew what the full, spelled-out terms meant! Unless they've had some prior medical schooling or instruction, most women and men trying to conceive learn an unfamiliar and unique language in their quest to see a BFP (big fat positive pregnancy test result).

5

THAT FIRST BFP

Through my many hours of Googling, I learned that of all couples trying to conceive, around thirty percent are able to get pregnant their first month of trying. Thirty percent can get pregnant practically as quickly as you can read this book! About sixty percent of couples get pregnant within three months of trying and eighty percent get pregnant within six months. A doctor once told me that you shouldn't start to worry or question fertility until you've been trying to conceive for over a year.

I had an inkling that I wouldn't be lucky enough to be included in that first thirty percent group, as I was sure coming off of the pill after taking it for a solid ten years would have some impact on our efforts. But, what do I know? I never expected it to take over a year, though. I never thought I'd have to look into contacting fertility specialists. From the time my husband and I decided to start trying for a baby, being the anal retentive and overly plan-obsessed person that I am, I diligently tracked each period, all ovulation days, and days that we tried to conceive. Each month we were let down when Aunt Flo would visit. If you're unfamiliar, having Aunt Flo visit is a less vivid way of saying having your period. I started to worry that there was something wrong with one of us and that we couldn't get pregnant. When we hit that one year mark, like the doctor mentioned, I scheduled an appointment with a specialist and so did my husband. I was going to have to get my downstairs region prodded and my husband was going to have to make love to a plastic cup. We had to find out if something was wrong. The appointments were scheduled.

It had been over a year of trying when I found out my period was late and I took my first at-home pregnancy test. There were two bold, blue lines! One line is negative, but two is a BFP! Needless to say, we didn't end up going to our appointments with the specialists. We dodged a bullet and were capable of getting pregnant. We got our first BFP!

The morning I took the first pregnancy test and saw the positive, I remember taking a picture of it and texting my mom to see if she saw it too. *Was it a defective test? Had I let it sit too long?* If you let a test sit too long, it could give a false positive by showing an evaporation line. No, there is no way I had let it sit too long. My mom was the first person I told and she seemed just as excited as I was. After I took additional tests, I knew it was real. It was February and by my calculations, I would give birth to our first baby in October.

To tell my husband the good news, I drafted up a letter with a photo of the test, because the thought of giving the test that I peed on to him seemed a little awkward at the time. That's funny, because there isn't a whole lot in life that makes me feel uncomfortable. Now that I think about it though, I have a feeling that he would have been so excited that the last thing on his mind would have been the fact that I peed on the stick he was holding. The letter I made ended with, "Baby Hahn, due October 2016." I placed it in an envelope and left it on the table with the other mail so that my husband would open it. I still laugh about what happened, because when he opened it, it didn't quite hit him. It didn't register and he was pretty confused. I thought I was being as obvious as I could. I didn't tiptoe around the news in the letter. Yet, he asked me, "Who sent this?" My cute idea had epically failed. I had to explain that I had put the letter together. Heck, it was my handwriting on the envelope! We were pregnant. It was our Baby Hahn that was due. I think he thought someone else in the family sent the letter and someone else was expecting a baby Hahn due in October, even though there wasn't a stamp or return address on the envelope. My husband is a pretty simple man, and I do love that about him. I should have just let him walk in the door and told him the good news, "Hey babe, I'm pregnant." Lesson learned for the future.

My husband and I had never been more excited and nervous in our entire lives. We have so much love for each other, and we wanted to share some of that with a little one (or two). By that point in February, I had become so discouraged, sad, jealous of friends, and almost gave up on our dream. It seems utterly ridiculous to me now that I was so close to giving up on something I wanted so desperately so early. If you want something and you know, deep in your heart that it's important to you, never give up.

As crazy as it sounds, before I found out I was pregnant, I felt like everyone around me was able to get pregnant, but we were the only ones incapable. I wasn't aware of anyone else that I knew who was trying but had been unsuccessful. Each pregnancy announcement that I would see, I would have to hide my disappointment and mask it with pure happiness for the couple. It finally happened for us though, and I thought our prayers had been answered. Good things take time, right? My husband and I want more than anything to become parents. After two more at-home tests to confirm I wasn't seeing things, I made an appointment with a local doctor. Even if I took multiple tests, at-home pregnancy tests can sometimes give false positives. With a clinic-administered urine and blood test, the doctor confirmed it. I was due October 2016!

October. Such a perfect month. My husband and I's anniversary is that month and I simply love that time of year. The air is crisp and cool. The leaves fall and nature is beautiful. Halloween preparations are in full swing. Trips to pumpkin patches or haunted houses are mandatory. Apple cider and all things pumpkin spice are available. The anticipation of having a little baby to dress up for Halloween was exciting. We could take adorable family portraits and select one for our Christmas card. What a wonderful second anniversary gift God was blessing us with! We felt lucky and everything seemed to be lining up according to expectation.

6

WHAT THE SYMPTOMS SAY

Being pregnant is exhilarating and scary when it's your first time. When I found out I was pregnant, I was only about five weeks along. I hadn't experienced any symptoms at that point, but I was highly anticipating their arrival. Crazy, right? Who looks forward to throwing up, headaches, or peeing constantly, just to name a few? Well, I did. My thought was that the more symptoms I experienced, the more reassurance that our pregnancy was progressing as it should.

I wouldn't know, because I've never felt a baby kick in my tummy, but from what women say and what I imagine, having a baby kick and feeling a new life develop inside of your body is beyond comprehension, changes your life, and is worth any discomfort along the way. A woman is born with one to two million eggs, way more eggs than a woman could ever possibly need. So, how does it work, in layman's terms without all the medical jargon? Ovulation happens around the middle of a woman's menstrual cycle, when an egg reaches maturity in one of her ovaries and is released. At that point, the egg gets sucked up into the nearest fallopian tube. This is prime time for conception, because the average egg only lives about twenty four hours. Whereas, sperm can live inside a woman's body for about five days. If a miracle happens and the egg meets up with a sperm, the egg continues its journey and makes its way to the uterus. If that miracle doesn't happen, the journey ends and having a baby that month is off the table. You have to try again next cycle. Pregnancy is different for every woman, and even differs for the same woman from one pregnancy to her next. That's an idea that has taken me some time to absorb. I couldn't just ask, "What happens next?" or "What does this mean?" because it's different for everyone. Some pregnancy symptoms last weeks, while others are only temporary and don't happen to everyone. As a pregnant woman, adjusting to the hormonal changes in your body causes a plethora of symptoms. In the first few weeks of pregnancy, changes on the outside won't be very visible, which makes it easy to keep pregnancy a secret, but so much is happening within the body.

As hormones rise, waves of nausea or vomiting can happen, and that is the infamous "morning sickness" we hear so much about. I never experienced this, which always made me a bit worrisome. Whenever I would question it, my doctor wouldn't seem the least bit concerned and would tell me that only seventy five percent of pregnant women experience morning sickness.

A fourth of pregnant women don't experience it. I'd say a fourth is a pretty big chunk, so that was reassuring.

The very first symptom I experienced was breast tenderness. Some days, they got sensitive and swollen to the point where even the slightest bump or touch caused pain. Next, my sense of smell started to heighten. If the trash wasn't taken out each day, it was almost unbearable to be in the kitchen. Normally, I let the trash go and take it out once a week or when the bag gets full. I don't smell a thing or if I do smell something faint, I just suck it up and wait until the bag is full. I'm all for only taking out the trash when the bag is completely full and not wasting garbage bags to take it out before that.

When I was pregnant, I remember the times when co-workers at the office would heat their lunches in the main open area and it would be as if a strong cloud of scent would hang in the air for hours, stagnant. Yet, I couldn't comment on it, because I was keeping a huge secret. It's not that what they were heating smelled bad, it was just that whatever it was they were heating was so potent. Normally, office smells don't faze me. They pass in about ten minutes, if they even bother me at all. My microwave usage in the office has been the reason for popcorn or heated chicken smell before. One time it was about ten in the morning and a co-worker heated up Ramen noodles. If you like Ramen at ten in the morning, more power to you. To each their own. Non-pregnant Nikki would never have been bothered by the smell, but something about being pregnant made me hate Ramen from that point forward and it made me feel queasy, especially in the morning.

Another symptom that showed itself early on was exhaustion. Before being pregnant I was pretty active running marathons, doing workout videos, and biking. I have a desk job but try to stay active in my spare time. I quit running and working out when I found out I was pregnant. I didn't want to take any chances, even though my doctor said if you were active before getting pregnant, you are welcome to continue your activities, but proceed with a bit of caution. Be smart and don't push yourself. In any case, I would still feel beyond tired by afternoon each day, and I hadn't done anything but sit on my butt all day, making occasional trips to the printer. As it turns out, your progesterone levels increase during pregnancy and that's what increases the sleepiness.

The fun (note my sarcasm) and common symptom of peeing frequently started when my uterus began growing, causing pressure on my bladder. Normally, I very rarely wake up in the middle of the night to go to the restroom, but when I was pregnant, I'd go at least twice each night. Your digestive system slows to increase absorption of nutrients for the new little baby growing inside of you, and symptoms of that are some lovely bloating and gas. The last physical symptom I dealt with quite often was headaches. I never get headaches, but when I was pregnant, they were a daily occurrence. With blood volume and circulation increasing, headaches are par for the course. You're pumping blood for two (or more) now.

Besides the physical changes during pregnancy, a woman's feelings will be like a roller coaster. I experienced mood swings, anxiety, happiness, sadness, but more than anything a heightened sense of empathy. TV commercials would bring me to tears, and I even remember crying over a radio contest. Our local radio station was having a contest to "win a new smile." A dentist in town wanted to donate his services to fix the lucky winner's smile and the radio host wanted to make sure that the station picked the most deserving contestant. Each day, listeners were welcome to enter the contest by calling in and explaining their story about how their teeth had been lost or damaged, or tell how their smile was embarrassing and made it difficult to function day to day. Contestants had to share how fixing their smile would improve their quality of life. Each caller had a sad story and brilliantly supported their cause of why they needed their teeth redone. I'd imagine the radio host only let the most convincing contestants actually talk on-air. Well, he selected well. I would cry every morning, listening to each story, no exception. A woman had such bad morning sickness during her four pregnancies that the acid from the vomit had corroded her teeth. Her teeth were in pretty sad shape after the fourth go-around of morning sickness. She was so embarrassed that she didn't want to be in any of the photos with her newest baby. Not only was she dealing with emotions and changes to her body postpartum, but her teeth had been ruined as a result. I cried. A veteran had bad teeth all of his life and since retiring from the service, hadn't had the opportunity or resources to get his teeth fixed and they were worsening. He made huge sacrifices for our country, but can't get dental assistance. I cried. I'd like to think that I'm normally a caring and sensitive person, but when I was pregnant, it escalated to the point where I was crying over other people's rotten or missing teeth.

7

TEST ADDICTION

Even though I was peeing all the time, crying over rotten teeth, and barely being able to handle trapping my boobs in a constricting bra for an entire day in order to look presentable in public, I was worried about whether or not I was still pregnant. Was everything going okay? I had never been pregnant before, so everything was new. It's not like I could look down, see into my stomach, and magically say, "Oh good, the baby is still okay." It's nerve-wracking not knowing what's going on. It's a feeling comparable to turning in a final exam in college and waiting by the computer the following days, stewing over the grade that might get posted. You think you rocked it, but you're just not sure. This was so much more important and serious than a college test, though. I was responsible for growing a life inside of my tummy.

When my husband and I were trying to get pregnant, I used a ridiculous amount of tests. I bought the cheap EBay brand ovulation strips for several months. They were made of a flimsy paper material and very small. I thought that if I knew the exact day I ovulated, I'd know whether or not we were trying to conceive on the best days. When seeing the second line on those was tricky and didn't seem to be helping much, I skipped straight to buying a digital fertility monitor and strips, despite the dent that made in my wallet. That was a square plastic unit with a screen. I put the test strips into the unit and it told me my ovulation information, displayed on a calendar and charts. The instructions said that it would take a few cycles for your device to "get to know" you, so the first two or three months of readings probably wouldn't be accurate or register at all. That's a lot of waiting, in my opinion. Well, when that option didn't seem to pan out either because ovulations days weren't showing up properly, I bought a digital ovulation kit. That kit was a box of several sticks that looked like pregnancy tests, but were digital and gave an ovulation reading shortly after they were peed on. If an empty circle popped up on the screen area, I wasn't ovulating. If a smiley face showed up, it was ovulation day. Of everything I tried, the Clearblue digital ovulation detectors were the most clear, seemingly accurate, and helpful in letting me know when I was ovulating and alerting me to the prime days for trying to conceive. I knew that the day a smiley face showed up on that detector, it was BD (baby dance) time. As you can tell, when something is important to me, I'm very dedicated and driven.

For a couple hundred dollars, you can purchase an electronic bracelet that monitors levels important to know about when trying to conceive. The bracelet is a fertility tracking device that identifies an average of five fertile days per cycle, doubling your chances to conceive. It eliminates the guesswork of timing BD days or actively tracking ovulation. All you have to do is wear the bracelet at night when you sleep. I never went so far as to purchase one of those, but it's pretty neat how technology is constantly advancing. There is so much help available. It's too bad that the amount of resources and support available for those trying to conceive doesn't match information and help available for those suffering from pregnancy loss. In any case, my husband and I made our plans carefully around ovulation days and I meticulously tracked everything during that year we were trying to conceive our first child.

After our BFP, my test addiction didn't stop. I was worried about my lack of morning sickness and stressed about the days when the symptoms weren't so bad. I'd think *why am I not miserable?* On those days, I wanted to take a pregnancy test to see the positive and reassure myself. Human chorionic gonadotrophin (HCG) is a hormone that is in a woman's blood beginning at time of conception. It's produced by the same cells that make the placenta and it's the reason that a positive shows up on pregnancy tests. HCG can be detected in your urine as soon as the first day of a missed period. The bolder the line on a pregnancy test, the higher the level of

HCG in your system. If you're experiencing a chemical pregnancy or if you're going to miscarry and you continue to take pregnancy tests, in theory the positives test results will start showing more faintly and will warn you that something is off. If you continue testing and the positive lines remain bold blue or pink depending on the brand of test you use, then it gives some reassurance.

Even during the beginning of pregnancy, you can get your blood drawn to monitor your HCG levels. When you're not pregnant, your HCG level is zero. In the beginning of pregnancy, levels of HCG are quite low. Soon, those levels start to double each day up until about week twelve, when it starts to decline or level out.

After all of my testing experience, I've learned that there is no benefit of testing like a mad woman. Yes, ovulation tests help tell you when you're ovulating, but those tests also put more stress on a couple to try to conceive on a specific day at a specific time. Stress doesn't help any situation. Once you see that BFP, one positive pregnancy test is all you need. It's unnecessary to test multiple times or again throughout your pregnancy. Again, doing that just compounds the tension of the situation. Let the pregnancy run its course. A nurse once told me, "Once you're pregnant, you're pregnant. There is no need to keep testing to reassure yourself." If something is wrong, you'll find out from your doctor, on your own you'll feel it in your body, or at an ultrasound appointment. Yes, fading positive tests may give you an indication that something is wrong, but you'll more than likely find out there's a problem from your body before you see anything on a fading test result.

This is comical coming from an avid tester and worry wart, but sometimes it's imperative that you try your hardest to simply have a little faith. Even if you're worried or nervous, trust in the process and trust what God has in store for you, whether that's good or bad.

8

PATIENCE IS A VIRTUE

When you're pregnant, you're told more than anything else, to wait. You wait for that smiley to show up on your ovulation predictor. You have to wait until your first day of a missed period, if not later, to take a pregnancy test. You wait three-or-so minutes to see a result on the test. After you finally get lucky enough to see a BFP, you can get a blood draw confirmation of pregnancy, but then have to wait until about week six to eight for an ultrasound. You are urged to wait until around week thirteen, when the first trimester at an end, to tell friends and family. You have to wait until week sixteen to twenty to find out the gender of your baby, if you choose to find out. Heck, the whole ordeal is a nine or more-month wait. For someone like me, who hates to wait, meticulously plans everything in my life, is anal retentive, and who is always prepared, waiting is not something easily done. Patience is a virtue.

Each week that went by, I analyzed myself in the mirror, looking for any indication of a bump that never ended up popping out. Sure, there was bloat, but that didn't count. After college, I gained some weight and was a little chunky pre-pregnancy, so I figured I wouldn't see much difference in my profile for a few weeks, unlike thinner women. Regardless, I would wait and wait for my baby bump to start showing every day. I had anticipated it. I downloaded apps on my phone to edit my belly pictures and to edit future baby photos. I wanted to add "My baby is the size of an apricot" labels and "Bump Ahead" captions to my photos. It was my first pregnancy. I was going to go all out and do all the things that first-time moms do. Saying that I was excited would be an understatement.

I was also impatient. My husband and I both were. At about nine to ten weeks pregnant, we decided to tell all of our close friends, family, and then about a week or so later, Facebook. When we announced, we found out that our best friends and my husband's sister were both due in October too, not to mention a handful of my other friends were expecting around that same time. It was a happy time for many of us. I remember celebrating my Birthday, thinking it was the last Birthday I'd have without children. My husband and I knew we were telling people a little bit before the recommended twelve to thirteen week time to wait before announcing, because miscarriage is so common in the first trimester. One in four known pregnancies is lost to miscarriage, but I never thought it would happen to us. I had a feeling I'd be one of those many lucky gals who have a beautiful and exciting pregnancy the very first time, resulting in a healthy bundle of joy my husband and I could spend our lives with and spoil the crap out of. Bad things happen to other people, but wouldn't happen to us. I was so naive.

9

CRAZY DREAMS AND SMELLY THINGS

Normally, I don't dream. Well, if I do, I don't remember anything about the dreams when I wake up the next morning. Pregnancy dreams, though, are out of this world. They're really something.

One night, I had a dream that we (I'm not sure who that includes) were back home where I grew up on the farm and my dad was changing the newspapers in the horse tank for baby chicks we were raising. I was a younger version of myself in this dream. When I was younger, my family kept baby chickens in the garage in an old horse tank that was peppered with holes, deeming it unusable for its intended purpose of holding water for livestock. Since it was retired from its original use, we used it for chicks. We'd house them in there until they were old enough to put in the coop with the rest of the brood. For some reason my chicken-raising memories had found their way into my dreams that night. A few minutes into my dream, I learned that the chicks had all died except for one. *Why was dad wasting his time and putting new newspapers in there if the chicks were gone?* I'm not sure. The lone survivor was black. I picked it up and asked if I could have it. Dad seemed helpless that all of them had passed away and only one was left, so he said I could. At that point, the chick started to morph in my hands. It began to look like a kitten. The black feathers took on a fluffy fur look. I asked what it was and dad said it was a fox. What was happening in this dream? I was holding a chick, kitten, and then a fox? That was the strangest fox I had ever seen! Then, multiple, giant sinkholes started surfacing and swallowing up the surrounding houses. Waves of water rushed out of the sinkholes and washed our driveway away – nothing else, only the driveway. How is that feasible? Again, I have no idea.

Out of seemingly nowhere, this woman I know, Bekah, showed up with a Bible, saying that her Bible journaling was way better than mine. It hurt my feelings that she would act in such an outright rude manner. In "awake life," I had gotten a Journaling Bible and was really into illustrating that every chance I could. A Journaling Bible is essentially a traditional Bible, but has two-inch or wider margins, sufficient for drawing or taking notes about verses. A Journaling Bible can either be an artistic outlet, or simply provide margins for notes. I've always loved drawing and since I discovered this idea, it gave me a channel to both doodle away and spend some quality time with God and His word. I woke up from that dream and lay there, processing the events that just happened as I slept. How strange.

Another night, I had a dream that we (again, I'm not sure who that includes) were on a cruise ship that had clear structuring, so that we could view sharks when at sea. Let me interject that if this was a real ship, I'd be on its first sailing. Anyway, there were rough seas and one night a wave crashed against the side of the ship really hard, taking me overboard. I'm not sure why I was pacing the decks at night all alone. Later in my dream, I asked how I had gotten back to land and "they" told me I had to be rescued. I must have blacked out through a lot of that, but I do remember seeing so many sharks. The sharks were the focus of my dream. I would just stare at them. They were the strangest looking creatures. They didn't even look like sharks, but in my dream, I somehow still knew what they were. No one would believe me when I said that the waves grabbed me and took me overboard. Everyone thought I jumped and wanted to place me on some sort of suicide watch. Right then, I woke up and was left pondering another weird dream, and smirking because I was loving pregnancy.

The last odd pregnancy dream I can remember having happened when we were camping. In my dream, my husband and I were at a wedding reception for an acquaintance. I don't care very much for this girl, so I'm not sure why I was at her wedding to begin with. If you live in a small town, everyone seems to know everyone else, so that is probably why. I didn't go to her wedding in real life. Maybe she was the center of my dream because I had surfed social media before falling asleep and that girl had posted something that appeared on my feed, being the last thing I saw before drifting off to slumber land. The food at this girl's reception included pulled pork sandwiches and baked beans. The venue was a structure that closely resembled a school cafeteria. My husband and I waited in line while a cook scooped food onto our styrofoam plates. I was appalled by how the cook was taste testing each scoop with the same spoon used to dish the beans onto guests' plates, as if the taste of the beans would change from one plate to the next. Then, when we got back to our table, my husband and I got into an intense fight, which is amusing to me, because we rarely fight. If we do, it consists of stating our frustration and then giving the other the silent treatment until one of us caves, talks again, and we pretend that nothing really transpired. Again, us fighting is extremely rare. My husband is beyond tolerant, so our lack of fighting is probably largely thanks to him. I don't even know what the tension in my dream was over. In the dream, apparently our fight was so traumatic that we decided right there at one of the reception tables to get a divorce. I woke up with tears falling down my cheeks. Despite being odd, the dream felt unbelievably real. I'd gladly continue to have strange dreams if that meant there was a healthy baby in my belly.

I touched on this a little bit already, but a wacky symptom of having a baby grow in my belly was a sensitive sniffer. A lot of women become more sensitive to smells when they become pregnant. Increased levels of estrogen can make every little scent hit you like a freight train. One night, my cat cuddled up on my chest and laid down. Her fur smelled strongly of vanilla frosting. There is no way she had come in contact with frosting or anything vanilla, because we didn't have any dessert items in our house at the time. I had been dieting pre-pregnancy, attempting to get back to college weight, and dessert items were a no-no. One day I was convinced that the back area of my office building stunk of strange dill pickles and mustard. Another day, I was giving my husband a hug goodbye before he headed off to work. He's so tall that his upper arm and shoulder is level with my nose when we hug. His arm smelled like Cheerios! This is strange on its own, but also strange because we've never bought Cheerios for the house. We don't even eat them. I have had Cheerios possibly one time in my entire life. If I tried, I couldn't tell you what they taste like.

When you're pregnant, it's like you smell things no one else can. One night I walked into the bedroom to get ready for bed and it reeked of poo. It was so incredibly strong that I thought actual particles of poo were entering my nostrils and sticking to my nose hairs. My husband was already lying in bed and I couldn't understand why he wasn't appalled by the stench. Even though I know he didn't, I jokingly asked if he farted. He said, "No." Then, I explained how I smelled poo. My husband looked at me and said, "That's just us, honey." Great. We stink. Que eye roll. We both started laughing. However, as I was changing into pajamas a few minutes later, I saw an itty bitty dog turd in my closet, a little bit hidden by some shoes. That was the culprit. Our Chihuahua is potty trained to a certain extent, but sometimes he is naughty and poops inside. That night was one of those naughty nights, but my husband hadn't seen or smelled the dog droppings. Our dog is a tiny Chihuahua, so his poops are teeny, but they can sometimes pack a punch when their smell hits your nose. Maybe our dog had done it hours prior. Who knows? Sometimes, the smells I encountered during pregnancy were really strong, but mostly I was just taking in the experience, excited about everything happening with the pregnancy.

10

BLINDSIDED

Our doctor recommended scheduling my first ultrasound after week eleven of pregnancy. I had only been nauseous one time during all of those weeks, but I had felt sore boobs, had been peeing ridiculously often, constantly felt exhausted, and had bad headaches every day of every week. I felt those things up until the doctor visit we had been so highly anticipating. I had no reason to think anything was abnormal. At the time, I had only known of one person that I was acquainted with who had suffered a miscarriage and she had suffered five before welcoming her beautiful baby girl into the world. I thought she had a rare issue that I'd never have to worry about. I was foolishly under the impression that miscarriage is rare. I had spent all of my time researching getting pregnant and pregnancy. It didn't occur to me to look into anything involving pregnancy loss at that point. I didn't think I'd ever need know too much about it.

My mom never had morning sickness and maybe I was part of that lucky twenty five percent of pregnant women who don't experience morning sickness. I was somewhat confident that everything was going to be fine. Symptoms were arising as they should. There wasn't much else I could monitor. My husband and I were planning what the nursery would look like, dreaming about our future, joking about what our kid would be like, tossing around baby names, and just enjoying the anticipation of becoming parents. I had ordered the jungle themed crib bedding for the nursery. It was going to be so special to be having a baby at the same time as some of our best friends and family. I should have been about twelve weeks along when we had our first ultrasound appointment. Now, let me back up a little. The doctor that I chose to go to has a specific schedule of when he likes to see patients throughout a "normal" pregnancy and a specific strategy as to when ultrasounds and certain tests should be done. This is partly because he thinks his strategy is the best plan of action, but also because most insurance policies only cover so much. My policy only covered two ultrasounds, so if we needed more than that, we'd need to pay full price for each additional ultrasound. They aren't cheap. To save patients the expense, my doctor schedules the two covered ultrasounds at specific points during pregnancy, when certain tests must be run and certain things need to be examined. I'll skip those details, though. I trusted in the process and the expert.

There were several times I held back when I was concerned and let a medical professional tell me what to do or how to feel, instead of trusting my gut and being more assertive with my worries or questions. I keep telling myself I will never be like that again. Yes, they may know what they're doing for the most part, but I won't be a pushover again. A mother's intuition is something to be trusted. I was made to wait until twelve weeks along to get any reassurance whatsoever that my pregnancy was viable and healthy. I know now, that is ridiculous and I should have insisted on something at around six to seven weeks, like many of my friends or ladies that I talked to on forums had done. If you're willing to pay for an early ultrasound and it's what you think is best, the doctor should allow it. When I asked, my doctor was unwilling and I didn't press the issue. In larger cities, if your doctor won't do an ultrasound for you, there are smaller businesses or clinics that specialize in ultrasounds; it's all they do. You can pay to have one done there. For those of us who live in small towns not anywhere near an ultrasound location like that, it's not an option. We waited until I passed the eleven-week mark. My husband and I went to our first ultrasound appointment anxious and excited. A small part of me was nervous, but it was only a speck of nerves because I'm a worry wart with everything, whether that be stressing about if I forgot to unplug my hair straightener before leaving the house or being on time for any obligation. Mostly, I was anticipating getting to see our little bean on the monitor and finally hear his or her heartbeat, just like in the movies. I had dreamed of such a moment. My husband stayed out in the waiting room while I got a flu shot and routine pap test. Those are normally painless little procedures where you don't feel more than a pinch, but both ended up being rather uncomfortable and a bit painful. Being pregnant heightens your sensitivity in several areas, but it was all worth it. I would have done anything for that baby.

After those routine procedures were completed, I went to the waiting room and got my husband. It was time. We were both smiling ear-to-ear. We walked to the ultrasound room together, hand-in-hand. I laid back on the table and the ultrasound technician put the cool gel on my belly. After she placed the wand mechanism on my stomach and glanced at the monitor, the technician immediately said, "I can tell you one thing. You're certainly nowhere near eleven or twelve weeks along," because she couldn't see much. She told us she needed to do a vaginal ultrasound. Okay, that was no problem. After I put on a hospital gown, we began the vaginal ultrasound. I was so confused by what I was seeing. Nothing resembled a baby like I had read the baby should look like at eleven to thirteen weeks. At this point, I began to get sincerely worried, but still not fully understanding what was happening. Maybe the lady was right and the estimated due date was just really off; I wasn't as far along as we thought, even though I had been meticulously tracking my periods and information for a year or more. After snapping some photos and taking some measurements, the tech seemed kind of off and quiet, but I thought she was deeply concentrating on doing her job. I've read several places that ultrasound technicians aren't legally allowed to tell you much about what is going on when they're conducting an ultrasound. Discussing the details is doctor's job. Maybe that explained her attitude. At that point, she mentioned she needed to get the doctor and she'd be right back. I still wasn't expecting any bad news. I thought maybe we'd just be having a November baby instead of an October baby.

After I got dressed, the doctor was at our door almost immediately. When he came in, the technician wasn't with him and he told my husband and I that he had been watching the scans from the other room. He was very professional and proceeded with a sense of tenderness. From there, what transpired is still a blur to me. I do know he told us there was no heartbeat, it looked like I was only about six and half weeks along, and he was ninety percent sure I had miscarried. A miscarriage is easiest explained as losing a baby before twenty weeks of pregnancy. What the doctor said meant that we had lost the baby five or six weeks ago. I could have known that dreaded information had I been more proactive and insisted on getting an ultrasound sooner. Knowing sooner wouldn't have eased the pain by any means, but thinking about the fact that I had been carrying our dead child inside of me for weeks made my stomach churn. The doctor was only ninety percent sure? What does that even mean? Either the baby was dead or it wasn't, and he had already said that there was no heartbeat. How was there a ten percent chance that I didn't have a miscarriage? I didn't ask him any questions. In that moment, the details didn't matter all that much. I was mad, confused, numb, sick...basically every negative emotion one can imagine. It wasn't his fault, so I didn't take it out on him. All I could do was weep.

I bawled uncontrollably and my husband held me in his arms. I didn't care that the doctor was still in the room. I didn't care who saw me or what they thought about me having a complete emotional breakdown. My dreams were shattered. My husband and I's world was turned upside down and I'd never really be the same. That may sound dramatic, but it's true. In that brief moment, all the plans we had been making were altered and my outlook on life and motherhood drastically changed. I knew from that moment on, interacting with our friends would be tricky for a while and different in the long run. I realized that when we let the secret out and told everyone what had happened, that we lost our baby, everyone would look at me differently, with clouded eyes full of pity. I wasn't embarrassed; that's not the word to use. More accurately, I felt jipped, ashamed with my body, and responsible. I was simply devastated and sharing that kind of pain with the world can be difficult. It's personal and sharing something of such importance makes you vulnerable. It's in human nature to avoid being vulnerable, so telling someone, anyone, that you lost your baby takes courage.

I felt like I had failed; like my husband had done his job, but my body messed up and the one thing that a female is supposed to be able to do in life my body wasn't able to accomplish. I knew that, for a while at least, any time I would see anything baby-related, I was going to want to cry or throw up. I was mad, too. *Why us, God?!* Why do people who make it clear to the world that they don't want kids get blessed with healthy babies, when some of us who try and try get the misfortune of losing a baby (or more than one in some cases)?! Why do people who actively

NICOLE HAHN

try to avoid having a child by using protection end up having "oops babies," yet some try for years without luck or end up with loss? My faith was certainly being tested. Suddenly, a gateway to another new world was opened up to my husband and I. This time it wasn't a world we wanted to be a part of. It was a world populated by those who had tried, struggled, and lost. Did you know that around six million pregnancies happen in the US each year? Of those six million, two million are lost. Of that lost two million, a whopping 600,000 result in miscarriages, 1.2 million sadly end in abortion, and 64,000 are ectopic pregnancies. Those are just estimates and numbers I found during my Googling quests, so their authenticity is questionable, but they still get the point across that the baby loss world isn't as small as I thought. Being freshly immersed into this world was like joining a club that you never want to be a part of, a club in which you never dream that you'll even be considered for membership. It's a club for losers. My husband and I became members whether we liked it or not. At that point, I hadn't paid the dues, but I would over time.

Continuing our story, something was still wrong. As if hearing the news that our baby was dead wasn't bad enough, the doctor wanted me to come back in forty eight hours to give more blood. The last thing I wanted to do was go back to that office for any reason or to revisit the pain, an office with a waiting room full of pregnant ladies, seeing something I wouldn't have in the near future, or maybe ever. Why did they need more blood from me, when we already knew it was a miscarriage? What happened, happened. I wanted everything to be

46

over so I could try to move on and deal with the loss. Couldn't they prescribe some medication to make the ordeal final? Nope. More blood and more doctor visits were in my future.

I was confused as to why I hadn't expelled anything yet. I hadn't bled one bit. Everything should have been fine, but it wasn't. I should have still had a healthy baby in my belly, but the doctor said I didn't. Since that awful appointment, I had almost feared going to the bathroom each time, scared that I'd officially lose it and it would all be real. I thought that was what was supposed to happen next; that I was supposed to bleed a lot.

It turns out all the giving of blood was to monitor my HCG levels, to see if they were decreasing, as was the natural progression with miscarriage. A nurse explained to me that normally, during a miscarriage your hormone levels go from very high healthy-pregnancy levels back down to zero at a drastic rate, and that's when your body expels the pregnancy. That's how miscarriage works. I hadn't done that, though. What more was wrong? Why was my body such a failure? It can't even miscarry properly. After the first couple of blood draws, results showed that my levels were still very high and staying stagnant.

In that case, my body wasn't doing what it was supposed to. I was scheduled for minor surgery to have what's called a D&C. A dilation and curettage procedure, or a surgical evacuation, is a minor surgical procedure where the doctor opens the cervix and scrapes the uterine lining with a curette to remove abnormal tissues (the baby and placenta in my case). It is a fairly simple procedure, but I had never had surgery before, so I was nervous, not to mention my emotions were running high. I was a mental and physical mess. I had a bad reaction to the anesthesia and some pain afterward, but the surgery itself was short and went as expected. After the D&C, it was official. I was no longer pregnant. Our baby was no longer there.

I'm a highly emotional person normally, so I don't deal with sad things or emotionally-charged situations all that well, whether that be a pet dying, getting a bad score on a test, or disappointing someone I love. I stress, stew, and make myself sick over the smallest things. I'm sensitive and I lean on my loved ones probably more than I should. All I could do the week following surgery was cry and I had a constant sick feeling (that wasn't a result of the D&C). I wasn't hungry for about two days. I wasn't sure how I was going to be able to be around my pregnant friends, so I avoided them. I think they avoided me too, because I'm sure they didn't know what to say. Their pregnancies were evolving perfectly, and I was no longer going to be a mom with them. I took one step at a time and started to pray that someday I would understand God's plan for us, because even to this day, I still don't know what that is. Do any of us really know what God has in store for us? Some of us think we have it all figured out, but do we really?

11

YOU HAVE THE RIGHT TO FEEL

If you've suffered a pregnancy loss, you'll have good days and you'll have bad days. Sometimes I believe my husband and I can get pregnant again and have a healthy pregnancy. I'm not about to give up on such a huge dream. Hard times pass and there must be some reason for our loss. There are numerous happy stories about living, healthy babies after miscarriage floating around out there. God is continually teaching me to appreciate what I'm given even more and bad days are merely tests. Some days I'm okay.

I'll admit that most days for a while though, I was not. I was the farthest thing from okay that there is. I wish I could be as strong as some of the women in my life. Sometimes I still get mad at myself over how much I struggle. That's right; I still have bad days where all I want to do is cry. Time has passed. Why can't I just act normal? I've read that women still have sad and emotional days years after loss. Everyone handles pregnancy loss differently. Some hide it, do their best to pretend it didn't happen, and put their blinders on and focus only on the future. I happen to be one of the women who has struggled immensely, constantly rehashing everything that happened in my mind.

There is an image that I saw one time that really struck me. It was a photo of a dog and her pup standing side by side. They had both trudged through some deep mud. The mud only came up to the dog's mid-leg, whereas the mud came up to the little puppy's neck. It illustrates how we may go through similar struggles, but some of us are affected differently. The answer to "How deep is the sludge?" depends on who you ask. On that same line of thought, it's important to note that thinking that you can't be sad because someone else in the world might be worse off is the same as thinking you don't deserve to be happy because someone else in the world might have it better. You have every right to feel, no matter how deep the mud is.

There will be so many days where you make it through, but are surprised by how. I wanted to be happy for all of my pregnant or new mommy friends, but most of the time I was just reminded of what my husband and I lost. I was constantly being surrounded by others who were moving forward in their lives and building a family, but we seemed to be stuck. Heck, maybe we were moving backwards, because losing babies and struggling with trying to conceive puts a strain on your relationship, without a doubt. Our marriage wasn't in danger by any means, but loss adds another dynamic and makes certain situations tough to handle. Not being happy for my friends may make me a horrible person, but it's something I couldn't help. I wanted so badly to be able to act normal, and on the outside I think I did a good job of that. However, I wanted to not be phased by any mention of baby-related things. I wanted to be able to joke again. It took a long while for that part of me to come back, so be patient if you haven't gotten there yet.

I was still sore for days after the D&C surgery, my head hurt, and I was emotionally overwhelmed. It was a struggle to act like everything was okay, because that's what you're supposed to do. If you suffer from a miscarriage, you're supposed to snap back and go through day-to-day activities as if nothing happened, like each day is a new day to start fresh. After a bit, people quit acknowledging that you were ever pregnant or lost a baby. Your baby never lived outside of your womb, so the miscarriage was no big deal, right? When people bring their babies around, you're supposed to smile and ask to hold it while making goo-goo noises and talking baby, even if that's the very last thing in the world you feel like doing. That's how we're supposed to act post miscarriage. Those ideas that culture pushes on us suck.

Like I said, you'll have good and bad days, and that is okay! It's okay to not be chipper and "fine" all the time. You hurt because you care. I'm tired of society pushing us to be quiet. No one should have to stay hush hush when they are hurting or when they have lost. Our babies matter, whether they lived outside of the womb or not. I got tired of staying quiet so that others could feel comfortable. Face it, some things in life will make you uncomfortable and that is just how it is. That's how we grow. John Shipp once said, "Ships in harbor are safe, but that's not what ships are built for." You never reach the fruit if you don't step out on a limb. Most simply put, you gain nothing by staying in your padded little comfort zone. A part of me was changed forever. That doesn't mean you have to avoid me or talk behind my back in hushed tones. I'll admit, some friendships have drifted apart because we don't know how to be around or talk to each other anymore, but the important relationships have strengthened and new friendships have developed. It may have taken some time for me to muster up courage to share something so intimately personal with the world, but I'll talk about my experience, because there is nothing to be ashamed of. I'm not afraid of those who say I shouldn't talk about it.

For me, some of the worst feelings came during follow up appointments. Sitting in the waiting room at the clinic, I would be surrounded by women with baby bumps or women with their children. It affected me more than I thought it would and it took every ounce of self-control not to start weeping in my chair. I'd reminisce about when I used to walk into that same waiting room with joyful anticipation. That feeling has been replaced with dread and hesitation. I loathe going to the doctor now, for any reason, not that I ever particularly enjoyed visiting the doctor. At post miscarriage follow-up appointments, I'd look at one of the women and wonder what my husband and I would be like at that stage of pregnancy. I'd watch a little kid messing around with the books in the waiting room and picture what our little one would have been like when they got to be that age, what book they would have wanted to grab off of that table. Would he or she have even been into books, like I am? My mind would wander.

I carefully navigated my way through each day and I was a damn good actress. Every day, numerous times, I get asked, "How are you?" My response is always, "I'm doing well. What about yourself?" and the individual will proceed to tell me about his or her day or respond in a cheerful way. If those people I interact with only knew how many times I lie in a day. Maybe they're lying too. It's all about formalities. How else would you start an interaction if it weren't with a cheerful greeting? Face it. No one actually cares how you're doing when they ask, except maybe your parent or spouse. I say that I'm fine, but the truth is, there are times I'm not. After a pregnancy loss, you'll often have a sad, empty feeling in the pit of your stomach, like you're missing something huge, and you are. Your baby is gone.

I watched a movie one time where a woman miscarried a baby that she didn't want. It was a pregnancy that happened by mistake and she was devastated when she found out she was expecting. She cried after the miscarriage and that confused me back when I saw the movie pre-loss. I didn't understand until now. I was confused why she was upset if she never wanted the baby in the first place. I hate to admit this, but I remember ignorantly thinking, "Isn't this a good thing, since you didn't want it?" Well, now that I know how it feels and I've read a lot of women's stories, I learned that women who lose an unwanted or unplanned pregnancy feel a unique form of heartache after miscarriage. I wouldn't know firsthand, because I very much wanted my babies, but I've learned that women who lose an unplanned or unwanted pregnancy get confused and upset just the same. Even if they didn't want to be pregnant, it's primal and inherent to want to reproduce. Part of being a woman is having the potential to be a mother. It's in our genes and we want that choice. We're programmed to procreate and even if we think we never want to have children, it gives our life purpose to know that we have the ability to have a baby if we choose. If the ability to have babies is taken away, it's unfair and confusing, leaving us stupefied. Even if a woman doesn't plan to have children, she still wants the comfort of knowing it's an option.

I still feel guilty that I couldn't save our baby. The realness hit me a while ago, of course, but our loss is still hard to swallow, and some days it's still raw. I tried to distract my mind, but nothing seemed to work. In the beginning I tried to stay strong, put on a smile, and not talk about it, for the sake of those around me. That's what I was supposed to do. Being sad and devastated, while trying to hide most of the time, was exhausting though. Dealing with pregnancy loss is beyond complicated. I appreciated when people cared and asked me how I was doing. In fact, most of the time I needed that and wanted people to care. I wanted people to acknowledge my baby. My loved ones were the only reason I was able to function during our first loss. On the other hand, I wish people knew that when I said I was fine, I wasn't, and to recognize when I needed some space. All I wanted was for them to either offer a hug or somehow magically say the perfect thing. A ridiculous request, I know.

Dealing with jealousy and self-loathing has been difficult. There seems to be a general understanding in the world that procreating is a part of life, so if you lose a baby, you feel like a screw up. If you look up "failure" in a thesaurus, "miscarriage" is one of the top synonyms listed. Even the word itself used to label losing a baby makes you feel like a complete and utter failure. "Miscarriage" literally implies that you've failed. You did something wrong. You carried your baby incorrectly and because of that, it's gone. That's what the word implies, and that stings. That sting might make you feel embarrassed or shameful. Please don't let those feelings crowd your heart for too long. They're liars. In the case of most miscarriages, there is nothing the woman could have done to save the baby.

There's a huge difference between saying something and believing it. I still try to tell myself that I'm not worthless; it wasn't my fault and we can have a kid someday. Our misfortunes are merely bumps in the road and are meant to make us better, stronger. God is testing and preparing us. Plenty of women have miscarriages and continue on to have healthy children. For the longest time, truthfully and deep down, I didn't believe a word of what I was trying to tell myself, no matter how hard I tried. I wanted to have hope, but it was very hard. You get in this funk where you feel hollow and hopeless, like nothing may ever work out in your favor ever again. Little things like your snack purchase getting stuck in the vending machine or getting a parking ticket makes you think to yourself, "Yep. Why not? My luck. This is how my life is going." Even if I didn't believe the words of optimism I tried to feed myself for a long time, I continued to tell myself positive things, for the mind is just like most living things. It eats and thrives on what you feed it.

I was so afraid, jealous, sad, and depressed. It took us a year to become pregnant the first time. Who knew if we could make it happen again! Some of my friends were having their second or third child. I'd be beyond thankful for one, and maybe that is what God was trying to teach me. Be more thankful for blessings. I couldn't help but feel jealous. Some of my friends tell me stories about going off birth control, getting pregnant in a matter of weeks or a couple of months, and having beautiful pregnancies. While I'd love to be only happy for them, I couldn't help but feel bitter toward them and bitter with God. Why couldn't my husband and I have been that lucky? I don't want my friends to struggle or be sad by any means, but I wish I could be as lucky as they seem to be. When my sister-in-law, who had been due the same week we were, shared the news of finding out the sex of their second baby, the first thought that came to my mind wasn't one of joy like it should have been. Instead, all I could think about was that we would have been finding out the sex of our little one right around that time too, but never would.

At one point post loss, I stumbled across a video online of a baby in the womb at seven weeks. It was amazing. It wasn't just an ultrasound photo, but a video of a little baby moving around and it was adorable. I felt a pull on my heart and I yearned so much to be a mother.

Still grieving, that video reminded me that I had life inside of me once. Today, I think to myself, "My body can start the baby-making process and make a life, but maybe it just needs some practice following through to the end." In the first weeks following the miscarriage, I was upset that my body failed me and I failed our baby. I felt like I had ruined it all. I was depressed. I have a bubbly personality and seem outgoing, so many wouldn't know how I was truly feeling if they saw me in public. I joke, act like a goof, and tend to handle stress pretty well from the outside looking in. Really though, in those first few months after the miscarriage, if I looked like I had pulled myself together and had it all figured out, inside I was actually still broken.

12

PRAYING FOR A RAINBOW AFTER RAIN

The hospital where I had my D&C does something really great for families who have lost babies. The hospital was gracious enough to have purchased a cemetery plot and stone for babies who have passed away before twenty weeks gestational age. If you've lost a child, you can arrange to retrieve their remains and do with them how you wish, but the hospital has their plot as an option. Given how young my husband and I are, we haven't reserved a plot of our own, and I didn't really want to have a tiny urn sitting around at home for pets to knock over and break. I wasn't sure having a constant visual reminder of that sort sitting around was such a great idea either. I don't want to forget, but I don't want that sort of memorial. For some, they want to honor their little one that way and that is completely okay. I get it. My husband and I didn't think that was the best option for us. We decided that utilizing the hospital's plot was the best decision for our angel. We continued to pray for healing and some resolve. The only thing we had to look forward to was the rainbow.

A rainbow baby is a tender and considerate term that is now so special to my husband and I. It's something that gives us hope. A rainbow baby is a child that a family is blessed with after the rain and storm; a baby that comes after pain and loss. It is the healthy bundle of joy for couples who have miscarried or lost a pregnancy at any stage. The first time I remember a rainbow coming up in the Bible is the rainbow that appears after the great flood in Genesis. God talks to Noah, promising hope and new beginnings. He says He'll never flood the Earth again. The rainbow was what Noah needed, the courage he desperately sought to be able to lead his family into new territory. Noah would never forget the past, but had faith and hope that the storm wouldn't come again.

I want to take a minute to discuss my thoughts on rainbow babies. If you're blessed with a rainbow baby, it's hard to tell people. For me, it was even nerve-wracking to tell my husband. One would think you'd be overjoyed to share such great news, but in reality it's terrifying. You've been down the road before, and it didn't end so great. You don't know if this journey will end the same way. It's fear of the unknown. Announcing your next pregnancy will leave you feeling scared and with a mixture of emotions ranging from joy to guilt. You'll want to be excited about being pregnant again, but at the same time you'll want to remember and respect the life or lives that you've lost.

That's a complicated balance to find. It's okay not to be excited. You've been hurt, so you know now that each day is a miracle, but please know that it's okay to make plans and have some hope for this new baby. Try to give that little bean a chance, as much of a chance as you gave your first pregnancy. The baby you're carrying deserves that love.

It's no joke that being pregnant again after loss is scary. Every tiny twinge of pain or symptom isn't "normal" to you. You'll worry if each little feeling is a precursor to miscarriage. Some will assume that you're "fixed" or all better once you have a new baby in your belly. They won't understand why you're still sad. Those people will never understand, unless they walk in your shoes someday. Ha - aren't they lucky to not have felt the things we miscarriage mamas have? Despite the mixture of feelings that a rainbow baby can bring, it's a surreal and exquisite gift. Take pregnancy one day at a time and trust God's plan.

Just over eight weeks since my procedure I wanted very much for my cycle and our life to get back to whatever "normal" is. I thought that I should have ovulated and had a period by then, but I hadn't. I thought, *if my body could just snap back and get back to the norm, that would help me cope.* I started to think that maybe I was an exception once again, one of those women that takes longer than usual to snap back. My doctor told me that if it takes longer than ten weeks to get a period after a miscarriage that I should give the clinic a call and be seen. I was approaching eight weeks and that seemed lengthy for how far along I had been when I miscarried. Maybe I was just impatient. On the other hand, a small part of me thought maybe I was pregnant again and that's why Aunt Flo hadn't visited. *Was this our Rainbow baby? What a miracle that would be! Already? So soon?* Although highly unlikely, it was possible and I couldn't help but put faith in that little twinge of hope I started to feel. God does miraculous things every day. I decided to take a pregnancy test one morning. It was a cheap, test-strip pregnancy test, and the result read negative.

Test addiction had struck again. I was expecting the negative result, because even if there was a chance that I was pregnant again, it would have been way too early to be detected by a test. I tested anyway. In any case, seeing the negative test still stung. It was yet another reminder of my husband and I's shattered dreams. It was just a pregnancy test. *Get over it, Nicole.* I did end up getting my period a couple of days after I took the negative pregnancy test. At least I knew my body was "working" again.

I know I shouldn't compare my life to others', because people put on masks and you only see the highlight reel of their lives, not the outtakes, but I can't help it. Social media and large social events continued to remind me that so many people around me were pregnant with healthy babies, but not us. When would we see our rainbow? How do you interact with people who want to talk about babies constantly, when all you feel like doing is escaping? I had been so naive in assuming getting pregnant or starting a family would be easy. How do you have hope for a rainbow baby after you've miscarried? There isn't a straightforward answer. My solution was having faith, staying distracted, and being optimistic about the rainbow after the storm.

13

TRAVELING THAT ROAD AGAIN

Three months had passed since we lost our October baby. We were planning to go on a trip with two of our good friends. They were some of our closest friends and are the couple who were due in October too. Her pregnancy was moving along beautifully and I was jealous, but I sucked it up because I was happy for her. I was in desperate need of a vacation. I was positive we could all have a fun time, without pregnancy needing to be at the center or even be brought up at all. Like I mentioned before, things were a bit awkward between her and I after my miscarriage, but some of that awkwardness wore off before the trip. Thank goodness, because the less awkwardness that still persisted, the better. I knew my time of the month was supposed to come the day that we left. I was excited, but also not highly anticipating certain aspects of the trip. Not only is traveling while on your period less than desirable, I was still not entirely sure how to act around pregnant women. I woke up the morning we were supposed to leave and Aunt Flow hadn't come. Impatient Nikki prematurely took a pregnancy test. It was negative. Another negative test. I wasn't surprised. I thought I was probably late and my body was still acting a bit funky after the D&C.

Days passed and by the end of our vacation, Aunt Flo still hadn't reared her ugly head. It is kind of rare for me to be four days late. Yet, I didn't think too deeply about it, because my body was still snapping back from the recent trauma it had experienced. Even knowing that, I took another pregnancy test the morning that we left the hotel to head home. I had thrown one in my bag at home when I packed before we left, just in case Aunt Flo didn't come. I don't know what I was thinking. Test addiction, again. I had a whole drawer-full of pregnancy tests and ovulation predictors at home just taking up space at that point, so why not throw one in? Those things expire, you know. Why not use them up? In the hotel bathroom, I sat there on the toilet while everyone else was asleep and watched as a faint second line appeared on the stick. I tried not to get too enthusiastic, because I'd seen those two lines before.

When I got home later that evening, I still was in shock. Maybe I was seeing things. That test I took was one of the cheap, unreliable ones. I took another line pregnancy test. The line was there again on a different brand of pregnancy test! I told myself that I would try a digital test in the morning and if that came out positive, I'd make an appointment with my doctor. The digital tests are far more sensitive, and thus more accurate. The digital test I took the next day was positive too. At that point, I was numb and not believing it. Again, I was trying to talk myself down and tell myself not to get excited just yet. The tests could all be false positives. I also immediately thought, "what if this bean doesn't make it either?" All of the "what-ifs" went through my head.

That was the same reaction my husband had. When I told him, I was hoping he'd be excited, but instead he was cautious and very straight forward. The morning I saw the positive test, we had decided to go to IHOP once everyone got up and moving and before starting the drive home. As we stood in line to be seated, I remember whispering to my husband and showing him the photo of the positive test that I had snapped on my phone. It was a little awkward, because we were trying to be quiet and not attract attention to our topic of conversation, but also awkward because I was a little surprised by his reaction. One of his first comments was that we shouldn't tell anyone until we are sure things are okay, which I agreed with. I would be lying if I said I wasn't a little disappointed by his reaction, though. I was scared too, but I was looking to him for some positivity and hope, since he's generally so great at being optimistic.

I called the doctor when I got to work the morning of the positive digital test result and the morning after we had returned from the trip. They thankfully had an appointment opening. For once, I wouldn't have to wait for something! The appointment was with a different doctor at a different office. This office is closer to work and home, and more practical overall. Plus, it didn't have any bad memories attached to it like the last office has now. I was happy with my decision to change doctors. After I met with him and my second pregnancy was confirmed, he explained that he was going to let me have an ultrasound at eight weeks, and then again at sixteen weeks, instead of at eleven to twelve and twenty six weeks. I would have some reassurance earlier this time and that was a relief. I was pregnant again and due on my birthday in March. I thought for sure that was some kind of sign from above. Baby and I could potentially share a Birthday.

After the wave of devastation that hit my parents when we lost our first baby, I didn't want to tell them we were pregnant again until I was more confident that it was a healthy pregnancy. I wanted to feel more confident before telling them. Keeping a secret from everyone is tricky, but keeping a secret from your parents when you're very close is especially difficult. Throughout the weeks to follow, it was hard not to explain to them or anyone why I was so tired, had headaches, or why I couldn't have a drink after a long, rough day at work. When dad would suggest it, I'd laugh it off and tell him, "Yeah, maybe I'll grab a shot of tequila or hang out with Jim Beam when I get home," fully aware that wasn't going to happen. When we'd meet friends at the bar, I got unique with my excuses as to why I couldn't or wouldn't drink with them when they offered to buy a beer or a round of shots.

Once again, my husband and I had a plan. We were going to visit my parents in Florida when I would be around sixteen weeks pregnant, well past the first trimester "safe" mark. By then I would have had an ultrasound and a couple of appointments under my belt, feeling more confident. I envisioned my parents being beyond ecstatic and I even found a really cute and clever way we wanted to announce it to them. My parents really like tumbler glasses to drink from, so I was going to get custom tumbler glasses made that read "Grandma/Grandpa established 2017." We wanted to share the good news to the rest of our friends when we returned from vacation by sharing a photo we had intended to snap at the beach. In the photo, my husband and I were going to be sitting on the sand, three pairs of flip flops (one pair a baby set, of course) dug into the sand next to us, and beside that there was going to be a clear baby bottle with an ultrasound photo situated inside.

Leading up to our first ultrasound appointment for baby number two, despite having ideas in my head of sharing the good news, I wasn't blissful or happy. I had the announcement ideas in my head merely because I'm a planner and having a plan is in my nature. Truthfully, I was a nervous wreck. That's what pregnancy loss does to you. It changes your entire outlook on pregnancy. At least it has for me.

During the next weeks, the fact that I was pregnant was pretty much ignored in our house. Men tend to internalize their feelings and I think my husband was scared from the moment I showed him the positive pregnancy test. So, we just didn't talk about it. It was the elephant in the room, something we weren't going to even acknowledge until after we saw that sticky bean on the monitor in the ultrasound room weeks later, and maybe not even right after that. I had my progesterone levels monitored, and they were on the very lowest end of the healthy range, causing me to begin taking vaginal progesterone suppositories twice a day, immediately. Again, I was willing to do whatever it took for my babies.

During the weeks we waited for the first ultrasound appointment, I attended my first baby shower since our loss. I'm embarrassed to admit that I was dreading it. Even though I was pregnant again, I was still grieving our last loss and I was so scared that I was going to get emotional, not be able to hide it, and end up embarrassing myself. But, I really wanted to go. It was for one of my best friends (the one we went on the mini vacation with), I was happy for her, and I always want to be a part of the big things in her life. How embarrassing would it be to completely break down right in the middle of my good friend's shower, though? I'm happy to tell you that, despite my fears, it ended up being pretty fun and I handled it better than I thought I would. I learned that sometimes you're stronger than you give yourself credit for. Things that seem scary or that you think are impossible, sometimes aren't that bad. I am so glad I went to her shower. I know I would be regretting it if I chose to stay home that day. On top of it all, my pregnant friend got me flowers on her day, because she knew it would be hard for me to be there. What a friend! She is a sweetheart. On a day where she should be reveling in her pregnancy bliss and celebrating her little baby, she thought of me. Little did she know, I needed those flowers and that thoughtfulness because I was dealing with a lot more than just coping with our first loss. I was terrified about being pregnant again. I had a lot on my plate.

The date of our first ultrasound for baby number two finally came. Based on my last menstrual period, we were thinking I was around eight weeks pregnant. When the tech did the abdominal ultrasound, he didn't see much and the screen looked pretty blurry. I expected as much, because it was very early. I knew a trans-vaginal ultrasound would tell us more. Regardless, I started to cry – cry from nerves, stress, and a blend of emotions. I was scared of history repeating itself and so far, the appointment was progressing very similarly to our experience with our first loss. The tech had me empty my bladder and then did the trans-vaginal ultrasound. Again, I couldn't decipher much on the monitor. He angled the monitor in my direction, and all I could see on the screen was the sac and some other blurry blobs, so I started crying more. I had researched what a seven or eight week ultrasound should look like, and that was not it.

To my surprise, the tech unintentionally looked at me like I was a loony and said, "Why are you crying?" His tone amused me, but I was far from being capable of laughing at the moment. He was legitimately confused. I said that I didn't know, only saying that because I didn't want to get into all of the details of why I was upset. I said, "There's nothing in there, is there?" as I was sobbing. He looked at me and genuinely said, "It's still very early. We more than likely won't see anything. This is normal." He mentioned that the sac looked good and was right where it should be. He also pointed and said some other things looked great. Everything appeared as it should for that stage of pregnancy.

The problem was that how things measured put me at about five weeks and two days pregnant, give or take a few days. That was the news that startled me. Was it possible to be three weeks off with our dates? Something to note, though, is that I have a strange cycle to begin with, and that was known even before my first pregnancy. I have about a thirty five to forty-day cycle. An average woman has a twenty-eight-day cycle. So, dating calculators used to estimate due dates for most women isn't going to work accurately with me. Also, I had used a digital ovulation predictor the month of conception and it told me I ovulated on a certain day. If the ovulation predictor was correct in predicting my ovulation day, the six weeks along was possible. Maybe we were just mixed up with our dates. Another appointment for an additional ultrasound in a couple of weeks was scheduled and more waiting ensued. Several days later and out of nowhere, I woke up feeling abnormally hopeful. I don't know what got into me that day. After what I had been through recently, I wasn't one for much positive thinking. Maybe it had something to do with a friend of mine, one of the very few who knew about our second pregnancy at that point, who kept urging me to keep my chin up and be happy about the baby. Surely bad news wouldn't strike again. She had been hosting a party selling children's' books, and I bought a couple that week. That's how peppy I had become. I was taking the first step of building our little nursery library for the baby. Having a solid book collection and little shelves full of books for our babies was something that had always been important to me.

Of course, the day came where I actually got a little spring in my step, got a little hopeful, tipped my chin up and started to be excited about the pregnancy, and our bad luck revisited. I went pee at around 6:00PM that chipper day and saw a little bit of brown, bloody mucus on the toilet paper. Naturally, I became a frantic, nervous, and upset mess. Since doctor offices aren't open in the evenings, normally in an emergency situation I would go straight to calling my mother. Mom always has the answer, or if she doesn't, she does a really great job of coming up with something to fix the situation. She didn't know yet, though. I had to take a different plan of action. I knew my husband wouldn't know what to do, so instead I immediately went to the pregnancy app on my phone to ask other ladies if they had experienced anything similar or if they had any insights. I also Googled "Brown Spotting." Yep, as per my generation's norm, I went to the internet. I even texted a nurse friend and my friend who has had multiple miscarriages. More than half of what I read was reassuring. Spotting or slightly bloody mucus is common between five to eight weeks of pregnancy. However, there were a few women that claimed brown mucus or spotting was the first sign of their miscarriage. They suggested keeping a close eye on it. Well, of course! As if I'd be able to brush it off right then. That's funny. In any case, I wasn't sure what was going on. I hadn't had anything like that happen with my first pregnancy.

Thinking back now, reading forums and things online in that situation is really silly. Every pregnancy is different, so something that may be normal for one person could be a bad indicator for someone else. In any case, even if every pregnancy is different, it was comforting to know other women had similar scares but ended up having healthy babies. In the moment, reading things on the internet was comforting. Even if what I read might have been false information, false comfort was better than intense stewing and fretting. Unfortunately, the spotting that began as some light brown on the toilet paper, turned heavier and became dark red the next day. I consider myself somewhat lucky in the fact that I have never had period cramps, so the pain I began feeling was pretty foreign. That awful day, the cramps started as slight twinges in my stomach, but gradually got more painful as the morning and afternoon progressed. Looking back, I'm not sure how I managed to stay at my desk at work, hiding what I was going through. When it comes to physical pain, I'd like to think that I can be a pretty tough cookie. As far as I know, no one suspected anything was different. I started to see some small clumps in the blood when I would pee and it was terrifying. I had heard of natural miscarriages and knew a little bit about what might happen, but I never knew it was so physically painful. With my last loss, I went in for surgery and the whole physical part of the escapade was over in a matter of hours. I naively thought that natural miscarriage was something that happened painlessly and then – poof – it was over quickly. Again, I was sadly mistaken. Miscarriages actually last days and are far from painless. Some women even lose too much blood and need to be taken to the emergency room. It can be a scary ordeal.

At around 2:00PM the day following the first sighting of blood, pain had reached its height. I went to the restroom, felt a strange pop midstream, and heard a plop. When I stood and looked into the bowl, I was mortified and overwhelmed. The past several times I had gone to the bathroom, there had been a lot of blood and a few clots, far more than any period I had ever experienced. That had been a lot to absorb on its own, but this time it was different. What I saw was awful. There it was, a giant clump that I tried not to look at too closely at first. I cried and knew that was it. I had just lost our baby in the public bathroom at my place of work. I had to flush my baby down the toilet like he/she was another piece of waste. What was I supposed to do, though? What do you do? When do you ever have the opportunity to learn how to handle a situation like that? I understand these details are all pretty displeasing, and what I did next is exceptionally disgusting, but I don't apologize for sharing. I reached in and picked it up. I was compelled to see it closer, as if seeing it in my hands would make the situation more real. I don't know what it all was and I don't care about the details. I held our second baby in my hand.

That evening after work I came home, sat on the couch, and for the first time in a few days, I felt numb and there was a disconcerting sense of calm. I no longer had a nervous feeling in my stomach, because what was done, was done. There was no more stressing or pacing. There wasn't a baby inside of me to fight for anymore. There was no further need for cursing at my phone, trying to get ahold of a nurse or my doctor. I wasn't frantically texting my husband or mother. Yes, I did end up calling my mom in hysterics that day and telling her that I had been pregnant again, but lost it. I needed her to be there for me. The fear was gone and I was just open for the pain. Our baby was gone and it was all over, once again. One step forward, five steps backward.

The whole week and especially that awful day, I had called my nurse several times. I primarily spoke with the nurse because my doctor himself never seemed available for phone calls. You'd think that in such a small town, at such a tiny clinic, that the doctor would be more reachable. Nope. After the last bout in the restroom, I called my nurse again and told her what had happened. She sadly let me know that there was nothing to do and we were, once again, left with no other option than to wait. You can't prevent miscarriage – plain and simple. The nurse said to keep the ultrasound appointment for the following day. Instead of getting to see our little baby, though, I knew the ultrasound was going to be a confirmation of what had been happening in the restroom and also to check to make sure I was physically doing okay after the miscarriage.

The nurse, bless her heart, told me to not give up on the pregnancy, but I knew. I knew that I had flushed our second baby down the toilet that day. Our rainbow baby went to heaven. I never thought I'd be the unlucky one out of four once, much less twice. Statistics are weird. They should be reassuring, because far more healthy babies are brought into the world than babies that are lost. Statistics may give you a fluffy pillow to lay your head on during your first pregnancy, but once loss has touched you, you realize you're part of that unlucky few and statistics sort of become your enemy. After our second loss, I had to start accepting that this whole pregnancy journey was something I wasn't able to craft to perfection. I couldn't slap it on a pottery wheel like a hunk of clay and mold it how I wanted. My body isn't a formula that I can plug in data and receive my desired outcome. I have no control over what happens next in life. I have to accept that things will and can happen, and I'll have to deal with them accordingly.

14

SMALL THINGS
AREN'T SO SMALL

Surgical adhesive residue. That is what broke me one morning. After my D&C surgery I had to have after our first loss, I got home and saw that they missed removing one of the sensor strips on my stomach. I ripped it off on my own, but couldn't get the gooey residue off of my skin. It was there for days. Each day I tried to scrub it off with vigor. I used several kinds of soap, nail polish remover, and any option in sight. Rationally, I know skin sheds and it wouldn't be there forever, but in my head I was beginning to think the dark residue was going to be a permanent tattoo. After a few days, I was finally successful in scrubbing it all off. When I had, I sat down in the shower and cried. *Why?* Why was I crying over having a clean, residue-free stomach?! How silly. I cried because none of this went how we had envisioned and the residue was a trigger. I didn't want to have surgery, period. If I had to have surgery, I would have preferred it been a C-section a few months later, resulting in a healthy bundle of baby bliss. I guess that lack of residue on my stomach was a visual representation of everything being "over."

I prayed for God to teach me how to be happy for others during that time. Every pregnancy announcement on social media was like a dagger to my heart. I wished I didn't feel that way. I wanted to be happy for them. I wanted to be happy in general. I missed that feeling. Happiness is a journey, not a destination, and it's what you make it. They say you choose to be happy. Well, I wasn't sure how to force myself to be happy. I wondered what the next step was in all this mess. You have to make an effort to stop letting the pain dominate your life and you need to find a new normal.

Almost three months after our second loss, my husband and I attended a college football game. We received our degree from the University of Nebraska Lincoln, were in the Cornhusker Marching Band, and were both born and raised in Nebraska. Husker football is more than important; it's part of life. We were pumped for the game and decided to make a stop at the bookstore beforehand to browse clothing and trinkets and maybe buy a thing or two. I was walking past a man who had a small table set up displaying a book he was promoting. I didn't want to stop and attempted to avoid eye contact, but he caught me and spouted out, "Have you heard about our mascot, Herbie Husker?" I didn't want to be rude and ignore him like everyone else seemed to be doing, so I answered, "No," as I stepped closer to his table, faking interest. Apparently it was a fun story about the history of our mascot. As I stepped up to his table and gestured to pick up a book he asked, "Do you have little ones?" A little bit caught off guard, I frowned and answered, "Nope. I don't." I was a little bummed out by having to admit to a stranger that I don't have living children. He obviously didn't realize what he had asked and assumed that I simply didn't have kids yet, not that we had been trying and struggling with starting our family. To my surprise, he said, "Well, you really need those for this book. Sorry." and dismissed me, in a sense. After he made that statement, he looked away and shifted his focus to the next person to walk by. He wanted nothing to do with me if I didn't have kids. How did he know I don't have little nieces, nephews, or friends with children that might be interested in the book? I thought the way he reacted to me was extremely rude. He just brushed me off and all but said, "If you don't have kids, you can keep walking." It was such a small, fairly insignificant remark and gesture, but it hurt. Small, but not so small, because it made me very sad. I wonder when little reminders of what our life is missing aren't going to sting so badly.

I remember our first social outing after a loss. It was a wedding out of town and I was feeling excited about it. I was expecting to go and see our friends, celebrate love, and have some fun at the reception. I thought it'd be a nice little escape from reality. Little did I know that ninety percent of our friends would bring their newborn. I didn't know people often brought their kids to weddings unless the child was part of the ceremony, since you are generally out late at the reception, well past a child's bedtime. Kids and babies seemed to be everywhere, though. On top of that, since having a kid is what was new in most of our friends' lives, not only were most of their kids there, but that seemed to be all they talked about. I didn't have anything to contribute, so I sat in silence, piping up with a forced laugh every once in a while so they knew I wasn't just sitting there dead in the chair. I wanted to appear fully present in the conversation, even if my mind was elsewhere. During the ceremony, all I could focus on was our friends holding and quieting their babies or our pregnant friends rubbing their bellies as they sat. Talk at the reception revolved around babies too. There was nothing I could or wanted to do about any of that, though. Why ruin everyone else's happiness, just because I am hurting? I never intended to be a party pooper, so I tried not to be one. I guess sometimes you have to let go and let God. That's exactly what I did. If this is what He planned, then there must be some end goal in mind.

Even a small thing like my first drink after our loss made me emotional. I wasn't a big alcohol drinker before the pregnancy, so not drinking for nine months or more wasn't going to be a struggle for me. In all honesty, I couldn't care less about alcohol. My first alcoholic beverage post miscarriage was depressing. I thought I needed it and thought I wanted it, but I remember taking the glass and after my first sip, trying my hardest to hold back tears. I wanted to numb some of my feelings, and alcohol would help that, but I didn't want to be drinking. I wanted to still be pregnant. One positive thing about my experience with loss is that no one questions why I am or am not drinking at the bar when we go out with friends anymore. If a girl isn't drinking in a bar, everyone usually jokes with her and makes "you must be preggers" comments. If I'm not drinking, no one dares ask if it's because I'm pregnant again. For them, it would be too awkward to approach the topic. Again, God forbid you do or say something outside of your comfort zone. Joking comments are no longer part of my "normal." The bar is one place I'm slightly thankful for people's fear of awkwardness. I can be myself, whether that's having a drink or downing a glass of water, and I don't have to answer any questions.

15

SOGGY IN THE RAIN

If I can tell you one thing with one hundred percent certainty, it's that I do not regret sharing our pregnancies with our friends, family, and the world when we did. I guess the reasoning behind waiting to tell people until the highest risk of miscarriage has passed is because, like I've hammered home, people don't like feeling uncomfortable. Sending out pregnancy announcements, just to have to turn around and tell everyone bad news a few days or weeks later is difficult. Some think it's embarrassing or too personal. I have always been a very open person, as you can tell from my honestly thus far, so I disagree. Celebration is best done in the company of others. Well, mourning can be too. Without the support of friends and family, getting through each day would have been unbearable. I can't imagine keeping such a secret and not being able to tell anyone about it. That would eat me up inside. The same reason people wait to announce their pregnancy in the early weeks (*what if we miscarry?*) is the same reason some don't (*what if we miscarry?*). To me, that risk is worth it.

After our first loss, I had a friend who works in the neonatal unit of a hospital send me a little care package that her hospital sends women who have miscarried. Another friend had some incredibly delicious, personalized Georgetown cupcakes delivered to our house. The hospital gave us a very tiny, crocheted baby blanket as a keepsake. A few friends sent me necklaces with angel wings or baby feet.

A newer friend was sweet enough to send a very special gift. It was a necklace with a dragonfly pendent. Why a dragon fly? Well, the necklace was accompanied by a very touching story that gave me comfort. The story takes place underwater at the sludgy bottom of a pond with a little colony of water bugs. The bugs were always very busy and rarely noticed when one from their colony would vanish. They would notice one of their own was missing, or they'd occasionally see one of their water bug friends climb up a Lily stalk to the surface of the water. They found it odd that their bug friends would just leave and never return, because they thought their fellow water bugs were all happy at the bottom of the pond. If they were happy, why would they leave? They were always baffled as to where the climbing bug would go and why it never came back. Once it reached the surface, it was gone.

One of the leaders of the water bugs had the idea that the next one to climb a Lily stalk needed to promise to report back and tell all the details about where they went and why. The whole colony promised. Days passed and finally the leader bug who made everyone promise found himself climbing a Lily stalk. Once he reached the surface, he ended up passing out on the pad. When he woke up, his whole body had changed. He had four wings and a brand new body. He fluttered his new wings and just like that he was hovering above the water. He had transitioned into a dragonfly. The new life was exhilarating. Flying through the air and soaring through the sky made him happier than he'd ever been.

He was so excited to stick to his promise and tell all of his water bug friends about this new place. However, when he went to dip down, the water's surface bounced him right back into the air. Since he was no longer a water bug, he couldn't join them down below and tell them all that he learned. He had wings now. He was no longer an expert water bug swimmer. He also realized that even if he could get down there, his friends would no longer recognize him in his new body. He knew he'd have to wait for when they'd become dragonflies too, and then they'd understand. With that, he fluttered off into his beautiful new world. My babies are dragonflies and I'm still a water bug. I may not understand why they left, but I'm comforted by the thought that they're happy in a better place.

It's not only the gifts that helped during tough times. Those were generous and greatly appreciated, but what both my husband and I needed during those times was to know we had people to lean on when we couldn't stand on our own. We had each other, but it can be difficult to comfort each other when you are both struggling with the same heartbreak. How do you be strong for someone else, when you can barely be strong for yourself?

Despite having all of that support, I felt alone. Most of my friends live out of town, my parents live states away, and the only family that live close is my husband's parents. Though, even if everyone I loved were right around the corner, I would've still felt alone. Our babies were gone and I was empty, alone with my thoughts all day, every day. There is only so much I could say to my husband. I felt like I had exhausted his ear after a while and talking about it caused him pain. That was the last thing I wanted to do. Also, they say if something hurts, stop touching it. With me continually bringing it up or being sad, that wasn't helping anyone move forward.

Something else that didn't help was all the mail and emails I received. Still to this day, months later, and even after unsubscribing to any baby or mom-related thing I've ever subscribed to, I receive weekly emails about deals on formula, baby clothes, diapers, etc. I even continue to receive boxes of formula samples in the mail. I inquired to several of those companies about why I still receive those things if I have unsubscribed. Some of the companies I contacted claimed it takes time to remove people from the mailing lists, which I understand to an extent. However, if they only knew how each "Congratulations! You're so many weeks pregnant. You should be thinking about this," hurts, maybe they'd put a rush on taking us women who have miscarried of their dang lists if they've made a point to contact them about being removed.

Months after our second loss, I remember sitting in my living room watching the events of the 2016 presidential election unfold. It was the evening of election day and Hillary Clinton was running against Donald Trump. A friend texted me, "It's like our country is in labor. In a few short hours we will find out if it's a boy or a girl." While that was a hilarious text, I couldn't help but mope a little bit. Even the USA was expecting.

Hurting is exhausting. Moping around in the rain of the storm is excruciating. Something was stolen from me after my first miscarriage, that worry-free anticipation of being pregnant - of having our first child in our arms instead of heaven. I may be lucky enough to get pregnant again someday and have a healthy baby, but I will never have a blissful, carefree and happy pregnancy. I'll never want a baby shower, because I'll be afraid that I'll lose the baby after being showered with gifts. One of the last things I ever want to do is return baby gifts after a loss. It's bad enough I currently have a spare bedroom that was envisioned as the nursery filled with a crib and baby items from my childhood that my parents dropped off in anticipation for baby. During future pregnancies, I may feel guilty for any happiness I feel, for celebrating and anticipating the arrival of a new baby when my other babies aren't here on Earth. I'll never want to throw a gender reveal party, because I don't want to get ahead of myself and get excited when I can possibly lose the baby. I may never take maternity photos, because I don't want that reminder if we lose it/them.

If I get pregnant again, I'll take every day of pregnancy as it comes, truly being grateful for each day that I'm graced with life in my belly, knowing that any day could be the last. So many of my friends are able to have two, three, or four babies, without a single worry or complication. They share weekly baby bump photos and share every exciting event of their pregnancies without a care in the world, or at least that's how they portray their lives. I had a friend announce to Facebook at only five weeks pregnant, and she was beyond elated. She didn't have a worry in the world. Why couldn't we have had that type of experience?! Why? I'm healthy. I rarely even catch a cold. The only thing that is even wrong with me is some seasonal allergies. Why is having a baby – really the one thing a woman is supposed to be able to do in life – the one thing my body won't allow? It makes me sick to my stomach. When I think about it too much, it literally feels like someone is clenching my heart and twisting it. That's when my only option is to look to God. He's the only one with the answers, even if He's unwilling to share those answers with me.

I'm at the prime age for starting a family, so that's why so many of my friends are pregnant or have small children. Before we were trying, maybe I didn't notice pregnancy announcements or babies as much because my focus was directed elsewhere. Post loss, I've become painfully aware of the fact that once you want something or something is taken from you, related things seem to pop up everywhere and you can't avoid them. It's like once you go on a diet, you see desserts all around and naughty cravings seem to taunt you at every turn.

I want my friends and family to be happy. I never want anyone to experience pregnancy loss, but whenever I see another pregnancy or birth announcement, there is an entire internal dialogue that I go through, "YAY! Oh, gosh. I love them. I'm so happy for them. That's great. Their family is so cute. Look at that cute announcement! I wish we had a cute little family like that, that I could have multiple kids. ...but we just have a dog and a cat. Our home is quiet. I miss our babies. Even though I knew they existed inside of me for only two or three months, I fell in love with them the minute I saw a positive pregnancy test. How can so many of my friends have kids and kids and kids and we can't even have one?! Why do we deserve this? To have dreams dangled in front of us, just to be ripped away. My husband is such a selfless and sweet soul. He doesn't deserve this." When your friend or family member is pregnant, it hurts. As much as you'd like to not admit to jealousy or pain in the wake of someone else's happiness, it's honest.

Like I've said, I have a bunch of friends who have recently announced their pregnancies or who are due around the same time I was. Some of my friends are just starting their lives as mothers to little babies. Some are right in the middle of pregnancy euphoria. Some are having gender reveal parties and showers. My next thoughts are for all of them.

I am so incredibly happy for you. I want to see your joy. I love seeing you chipper, jubilant, and healthy, because I would never wish the pain of loss of any sort on anyone, especially those near and dear to my heart. Please remember that before anything else, I'm your friend and you are important to me. I know my situation makes you feel awkward. Sometimes I feel awkward about it, too. It makes a lot of people feel uncomfortable. You probably have no idea how to sift through this situation or what to say to me. You don't know if you should share things with me at all. I know you're careful not to say the wrong thing and upset me, but you don't want to leave me out of the loop at the same time. It's tricky. Where do you find the balance? I have no idea, but know that I understand your dilemma.

I know you'd never hurt me on purpose. There will be times when I'll really be struggling. It's not because I don't want you to be happy or that I'm angry at you. It's simply that I will often be reminded of what my husband and I lost and that makes me sad. I'll be jealous, too. I'll be sad for the babies that God needed back from my husband and I and I'll be depressed that you and I are even placed in this kind of situation, a position where we are forced to act awkwardly around each other when we never did before.

I'll be ashamed and disappointed with myself that being at your shower or gender reveal party will be tough. I shouldn't be thinking of myself on your day. I'll be embarrassed and mad at myself that instead of being fully present and supportive during the biggest moments of your life, I will be experiencing pain and questioning what I've been through instead. I'll unconsciously be feeling selfish, which I'll realize after the fact. I also know that it's not all about me. Others certainly aren't always thinking, "Gee, I hope Nikki is okay with this." Heck, how I feel might actually be the very last thing on anyone's mind.

I want you to know that all of that doesn't mean that I don't want you to hang out with me, show me photos, or share your journey with me. There will just be days when I need some space and I need you to understand why. Most of the time, though, I don't want things to change and I still want my friend. I don't want you to shut me out in attempt to not hurt me. Treat me the way you usually would. Tease me a little and text me about all of your TMI moments, but maybe show a little sprinkling of sensitivity as you do. Sometimes it will hurt to see your growing baby bump photos and it'll sting to see the shared album of your child's newborn photos. Being around your little one for the first time will be a huge deal for me and it'll be interesting to see how I handle it. But, what would hurt most is to not get to be a part of your life, to be outcast and lose my friends.

In some way, I know God uses us miscarriage mamas as small reminders to pregnant couples or pregnant women to not take a single second for granted, for you've been blessed with something very special. So, dear friend, your story and mine have drastically different plots and endings, but we can learn from each other's experiences – through devastating heartbreak and breathtaking joys.

16

PRAYING AND FEELING GUILTY

When I pray, I pray for a lot of things. I don't get down on two knees, intertwine my fingers, close my eyes, and verbalize my prayers, but I do lie in bed at night, shut my eyes, and talk to God in my mind. He can hear me, even if I don't say it out loud. I believe that prayer does matter.

I pray for peace for the world. The world is hurting so much lately — more than ever, I think. There is so much violence, misunderstanding, and heartbreak. I pray for my friend who lost her baby at six months pregnant and continues to struggle with medical issues. She is the most selfless and compassionate human being I have ever met. I pray for my grandmother, that she continues to have good health, be kind, and not be lonely. I pray for my parents, that they have good luck with their investments, not feel lonely, and be happy. I pray for my friends, that they keep their faith and persevere over any obstacles in their way. I pray for my husband, that he will someday be able to work his dream job, that he continues to have good health, and overall that he is happy. I pray for my pets, that they don't feel too sad when we leave them at home when we head off to work all day and that they don't take it too personally when I yell at them for being under foot when I'm scrambling around in the kitchen. I take moments to thank God for the good that He does, because behind all of the heartache we may go through, God is always good.

However, throughout our pregnancy loss experience, I've prayed more for myself than anything mentioned above and I feel guilty about that. I've been praying every day, sometimes more than once, that God blesses us with a rainbow baby someday. I feel almost like I'm begging, acting spoiled and selfish, as if a rainbow is something I deserve and if God doesn't present us with that, he's a bad God. That's not what I believe, but it's how I feel like I'm acting when I constantly pray for myself. Do you ever feel selfish when you pray? I'd like to think I'm not the only one. I pray for others and thank God, yet my wants and requests for myself still seem selfish. Maybe I need to work on establishing a better balance. I need to give more and be more thankful. That way, when I seek God's guidance or when I do ask for help, healing, or resolve, I won't feel so guilty about it.

Some wonder if prayer even does anything. What does praying do? This idea could be made into a book on its own, so I want to only briefly touch on this. I think the purpose of praying is greatly misunderstood. Why do we pray? The disciples asked that question first, so those who are curious aren't alone in wondering if prayer actually works. On social media one time, someone commented on a sad status, "my prayers are with you," and another friend of mine attacked her for making that comment. He questioned what good my friend saying a prayer was going to do for the situation. A prayer from someone miles away wasn't going to fix the problem that had already happened. The true purpose of praying is to connect with God, so in that sense prayer is always a good and a beneficial practice. We shouldn't pray only to get something in return from God. He doesn't run a fast food restaurant where we approach His counter and demand what we want. That's not how it should work. I try to think of praying as checking in with a friend and saying thank you, all while being humble and respectful to a being that is so great it's almost inconceivable.

Prayers aren't magical. They're simple conversations. Praying isn't like rubbing the bottle and summoning God, as if he's a genie or something. If we reach out to Him, He doesn't magically appear and solve all of our problems. He is wise. He takes into consideration our circumstances and thinks through the consequences His actions might cause. Remember, it's His plan that prevails, not ours. When we pray, it's okay to make pleas, but never demands. Remember that prayer is for our benefit, not God's. He doesn't answer to us. We are at His will.

17

HEALTH CARE PROVIDERS

Bedside manner is important, but I understand how healthcare providers see misfortunes like miscarriage so frequently that they become immune to the impact those things have. Everything can seem like another textbook medical experience and nurses or doctors can come off as insensitive.

However, an expectation I have for health care professionals is to have the proper experience or training needed to deal with delicate situations like pregnancy loss. That's not always the case. I was an English major in college, so I don't know, but don't they teach things like that when you specialize in medicine?

Dear Mr. Health Care Provider, when you tell a woman she lost her baby and then go home at night to have supper and sit on your couch without a care in the world as you Netflix your evening away, she goes home, weeps, and feels lost for weeks, months. Most of the doctors or nurses I have encountered seem so compassionless and cold. I'm not saying that's how all providers are. I'm not intending to lump all doctors and nurses together in that category. It just so happens that the ones I've had contact with have fit that mold. They acted like I was just another appointment to get out of their door. As upset as this treatment makes me, I can't blame them. They're used to it and maybe there isn't an instruction manual on how to properly deal with the feelings of women who have miscarried. Each woman's reactions and ways of coping are drastically different too, so that doesn't help either. Maybe some women prefer being treated like pregnancy loss isn't earth-shattering. Medical professionals do have to maintain a certain level of professionalism that doesn't leave all that much room for expressing compassion. It's funny how their actions can aggravate me, yet at the same time I understand why they act the way they do.

There were times throughout my appointments for our miscarriages that I was flabbergasted by things that were said or what transpired. The one that takes the cake is the phlebotomist that I saw after our second loss. A couple of days after that miscarriage, the doctor wanted me to give blood to check and make sure that my HCG levels had gone down to zero, or were at least getting there. So, this next bit happened only a couple of days after our loss, when the wound was still extremely fresh.

When I got to the hospital that morning, I made my way to the lab and the tech greeted me, "Come right in here. Oh, you're pregnant? Congratulations." She said this as she held my open file, documenting my medical history.

In attempt to hide my reaction, I simply replied, "I was..."
She said, "Oh, so you lost it?" Dumbfounded by what
seemed like such a stupid question, all I could manage
to say was, "Yes." She went further, "Miscarriage?"
No, the magic pregnancy stealing fairy took it. Que eye
roll. I said, "Yes." Not getting the hint from my one-
word responses, the gal continued, "Was it your first?"
I told her, "No. Second." She pepped up even more and
cheerfully replied, "Oh, how old is your first child?" Oh
dear lord. This was the misunderstanding of the century.
Was she really asking that?! I said, "We lost that one
too," and clarified my statement with, "This is my second
miscarriage." Unaffected, she asked, "Do you mind me
asking how many weeks you were?" Why does that matter
to you? Why does it matter at all? I didn't want to talk to
her anymore, so I said, "We weren't sure," in attempt to
shut her up. She didn't stop talking, "Then, are they just
checking your HCG levels?" Yep, that's what it says right
there on my paperwork you're looking at but apparently
not reading. Could she not read? Trying to not to be
rude and take out my frustration on her I said, "Yes."
That is when I started to get really irritated, because she
went on to say, "I have four children." I must have given
her the strangest, most confused look. Why would she
say that?! Was she rubbing it in my face that she was able
to have not only one, but four children? Cool. Note my
sarcasm. She continued, "I know how you feel. I had to
have this test done." That really got my blood boiling.
Containing my anger was becoming very difficult. You
have no idea how I feel, lady! You have four kids and
you've never lost one! When I didn't have a comment to

her statement, she felt like she needed to clarify, "I bled a lot with my last pregnancy, so they had me do this test to make sure my levels were okay. They were," and she shrugged. She actually shrugged her shoulders! I was in awe at this point. What the hell was I supposed to say?! Congratulations? Great, I'm so glad you've been so blessed?! I quit acknowledging anything she would say after that point. I wanted to run. She had taken my blood, was simply labeling the vials, and I was ready to get the heck out of there. I was ready to go the minute I stepped foot in the hospital, actually. All I needed was a wrap for where the needle pierced the skin on my arm and for her to put up the arm of the chair so I could get out.

Surprisingly, I didn't cry as I walked to my car after that incident. I didn't cry on the way home, either. Had that situation occurred a day or so prior, I would have been bawling like a baby. That day, though, I think I was so astonished at her boldness and insensitivity, that it took a while to let it all sink in. How can someone be so insensitive? A conversation like that should never have taken place with someone who has had a miscarriage, much less with someone who miscarried only the week prior. Shouldn't health care professionals read a chart before they greet a patient and begin working with them? Shouldn't they be at least a little bit informed? I was to the point where I was just unbearably sad. I don't think my tear ducts could physically produce anymore tears and maybe that was another reason why I didn't cry after that encounter. I wasn't sure I could mentally or physically feel any more sadness, even though I realize now that things can always be worse.

Post miscarriage the second time around, I got frustrated because I had so many people telling me different things. Friends who have had miscarriages were appalled by my doctors' lack of concern with my condition as it was transpiring. With my second miscarriage, my doctor didn't want me to come into the clinic, didn't want to check my hormone levels, and wasn't concerned about seemingly anything. His attitude made me feel as if he was looking me in the eye saying, "It happened once. Here we go again. Relax." I felt largely ignored and unheard. All he ever said was to wait and my questions were rarely answered. My concerns were left to fester. The doctor and nurses made me feel like I was overreacting or being impatient. This is my child. I'm not going to sit around when I can be doing everything in my power to save him or her. I wasn't told to go to the emergency room or get an ultrasound. The doctor was content in the fact that there was nothing to do to save my baby. I just waited, and each time I waited it was the most grueling, gut-wrenching experience.

On the flip side, I had the most pleasant experience with a dental hygienist a couple of months after my second miscarriage. She isn't a medical professional in the sense that she is a nurse or doctor, but she works with people's physical health and personal hygiene every day. That day, I left the dentist office feeling understood and worthy of someone's time. Everyone in that office truly listened when I spoke and weren't just trying to push me out the door. I wasn't there for a therapy session; I just needed my teeth cleaned. For once though, someone I had an appointment with somewhat understood my situation and feelings, or at least knew how to show some sensitivity.

The visit was my first appointment at a new dental office and part of initial visits involve filling out paperwork and documenting a lot of allergies or surgeries. I had to put down the information about my D&C procedure. When the hygienist took me back to the room, she started going over the information I had filled out. When she reached the surgeries-in-the-past-year section, she looked at me with warm eyes. Her eyes weren't full of pity like I had expected and had become used to, but instead I saw understanding, kindness, and empathy. Instead of rushing through all of my history, she took a minute to swivel her chair away from the computer screen to face me, touch me on the shoulder, and sincerely say, "I'm so sorry. That must have been difficult." She told me that she hadn't experienced pregnancy loss, but she struggled with infertility for several years. She proceeded to tell me that she was sure that it will happen for us some day and we should "keep pluggin' away." I loved that she was caring and made simple comments, yet worked a little bit of appropriate humor into her interaction with me. She was never pushy or overbearing. It was like she knew just what to say.

As part of my initial appointment at the dentist, I had to get new X-rays taken of my teeth. The hygienist wanted to be safe and was probably required to ask, "You're not pregnant now, are you?" I of course answered, "No." I wished I was. Over the years, standard advice has been to avoid X-rays during pregnancy at all cost, as radiation could reach the baby. The hygienist proceeded to tell me that they'd need to retake the X-rays periodically, maybe only yearly, but added, "Hopefully I won't be able to take them for you next time." I looked at her quizzically. She added, "Hopefully next visit you'll be pregnant." That put a smile on my face. This woman that I had just met had a firm faith in my dream and overall considerate demeanor. It was refreshing. Someone was on my side.

Like I said, not all health professionals should be lumped into the same insensitive category, but most of them can be rather crass. How a woman is treated post miscarriage can have a huge impact on how she heals. She is able to move forward more quickly if she isn't struggling with mistreatment from her healthcare providers. Poor treatment compounds the grief and sadness.

18

DON'T SAY IT

It's surprising to see who comes out of the woodwork to be there for you and who doesn't. Sometimes that surprise hurts. Those friends you thought were your sturdy foundation disappear, but you also gain new friends through the experience. The way you view the world has changed, and therefore you may connect differently with those around you. You may feel more at-home with a new group of people who understand what you're going through. If I have a good day, I wish people wouldn't assume that I'm all fixed. If I'm having an awful day, I wish people wouldn't assume that I'm irrational, unhinged, and need to get over it.

Those of us who have suffered pregnancy loss aren't treated with the same tenderness as parents who have lost a child that lived outside of mom. We're treated much differently than anyone who has lost a loved one, period. To those who haven't had much experience with miscarriage, it can be a challenge to understand the connection and instantaneous love that is felt for a baby that a mom or dad was about to bring into the world. Just think about a heartbroken sister or grieving widow at a funeral for their loved one. Comments that some say to those of us who have miscarried - imagine how the heartbroken sister or grieving widow would react to them? "It's for the best" "It's very common." "You can try again." What if you told that grieving widow that she'll be fine when she finds a replacement husband, as if the second husband will erase any pain left by the loss of the first. She can try again. What if you told that heartbroken sister that after a few years pass, the pain will go away and she'll find a friend to replace the void that her sister left. Unthinkable, right? So, why would someone think it's acceptable or helpful in any way to say those things to someone who has suffered a pregnancy loss? Loss is loss.

As I've mentioned so many times you're probably tired of reading it, discussing pregnancy loss makes most people feel uncomfortable. It's taboo. I think part of it is we fear what can't be "fixed." Even though I believe a baby is a baby at conception, some can't comprehend how something you've never held in your arms could be considered a baby. There are huge debates about when a soul actually enters a body or when a fetus becomes a baby. Also, there aren't legal steps required for miscarriage like there are for a birth or death certificate. For a miscarriage, you don't write an obituary notice and there is no memorial service or funeral. The truth is, my babies' lives were a part of me. I lost a part of myself each time a baby went to heaven.

I think miscarriage isn't discussed in part because the words used in correlation with miscarriage or pregnancy loss are so ugly and unappealing. They're terms that include "blood," "clots," and "cramps." Well, let's stop sugar coating life, hiding what we think is "ugly." Too much sugar will rot your teeth. It's ironic that it's acceptable to be so open about being saved by Christ, take communion, and imagine Christ's bloody hands and feet nailed to a cross in church. Heck, Christ's bloody image is often displayed in churches. Yet, we're embarrassed to talk about our own blood and physical condition when it comes to pregnancy loss. We can discuss illnesses and deaths of adults, but pregnancy loss scares the crap out of a lot of us. Infant loss and miscarriage scares us because innocent little babies aren't supposed to die. I will never completely understand how sins and ugly acts are okay to preach about in a place of worship, yet it's still taboo to talk about pregnancy loss even outside of a church setting. Our babies deserve acknowledgement.

People often don't know what to say to someone who is suffering such a unique kind of heartbreak and complicated loss. To be honest, presented with a situation where I needed to confront a woman who had experienced miscarriage, I would probably be just as conflicted had I not been through what I have been through. How are we supposed to know if it's rarely talked about? Since I have experienced multiple losses, I've certainly had my fair share of experiences with comments that are NOT compassionate or supportive.

This next section may make me seem like a hypersensitive cry baby that can't handle a single comment. Maybe that's accurate, but more accurately, I want to share how what you say may come off as insensitive. Here are eight things I highly discourage saying to someone who has suffered through pregnancy loss:

1. In attempt to comfort me, a couple people told me, "Be thankful that you weren't further along." That is not comforting at all. I'm devastated about losing children, no matter how far along I was. They were little lives, not little losses. My husband and I still made plans and had dreams each pregnancy. I still went through the pregnancy symptoms for months and suffered the physical symptoms of miscarriage. There was life inside of me. If anything, that comment makes me angry. I will cope and learn to accept what happened, but don't tell me that I should be thankful for something so miserable.

2. "It's for the best. Obviously, something was wrong." Miscarriage is never for the best. I know your intentions are to make me see that there is some good reason that this happened, but I see very little good in these circumstances. Also, bringing to light the fact that something was wrong with my babies, that nature was taking care of a problem, doesn't ease any pain. A related comment someone told me once was, "It's better than having a baby with complications." I have no way of knowing what my children would have

been like or if they would have had mental or physical issues. Saying that is assuming I would have cared less for my babies if they had been born with developmental challenges. False. I would have loved the stuffing out of them. Comments like that also support the absurd idea that a life is only valuable if it comes in a perfect package with a big shiny bow.

3. "Everything happens for a reason." Really? What's the super great reason for us losing our babies?! Please enlighten me, because I'd love to know. I truly would. Why did God let me get pregnant to begin with, if it was all going to be stripped from us in the end? What is the path that God is taking us on that is supposedly so much better, since you seem to know and are so confident? Those are all questions that I've asked myself. So, when you say with confidence that everything happens for a reason, please let me in on the secret that I haven't been able to figure out. I believe that God has a plan, but I also believe that sometimes bad things just happen. As you can tell, that comment doesn't evoke any warm or fuzzy feelings of comfort from this lady.

4. Please don't tell a story that you think is worse in order to make me feel better. Knowing about someone else's struggles or hearing about how someone else has suffered doesn't make me feel better. It makes me sad that others have encountered a similar pain, or possibly worse pain.

5. "At least you are capable of getting pregnant." Having a chance and being blessed with life in my belly just to have it ripped away is better than not being able to get pregnant?! Both are awful, losing a child and dealing with infertility. To be honest though, I'd rather still be trying to conceive than have to suffer through losing babies.

6. "It'll be okay. You can get pregnant again right away." Maybe I can't. Before this book, some of my friends and acquaintances weren't aware that it took me a long time to get pregnant the first time. For many women, getting pregnant isn't simple and all rainbows and butterflies. For some, it doesn't just happen when you wish. Also, gee thanks, I had no idea that children were so replaceable in your opinion. "You can have more," infuriates me. Oh, I can just have another baby and it'll be as if nothing bad ever happened? It'll be as if my last two baby's existences didn't matter? I can just have another one to replace them? Not quite, no. I don't want more to replace them. I wanted the ones we had.

7. "It wasn't your time." That does not help in the slightest way. Saying that makes me question fate and karma, and I've done enough of that on my own without your nudging. I'm twenty six, financially stable, healthy, and happily married. Why is now not my time?! How much better prepared can one be?! Do you happen to know the plan God has for me, then? After a pregnancy loss, your faith is already wavering and being

tested. Comments that throw that confusion and uncertainty even further off balance don't help.

8. "It's very common and a lot of people go through it. You'll be fine." Oh, I'll be fine because it's so common? Having miscarriages is just like catching the common cold, something unfortunate that doesn't feel the best in the moment, but passes and happens to everyone at some point? No. Just because it may happen to other women doesn't mean it's the same situation, has less of an impact, or hurts less. Not one bit. Knowing that other people suffer doesn't console me or lessen my own pain. If someone gets cancer, you don't tell them they'll be fine because lots of people get cancer. I don't mean to say miscarriage is anything like cancer, but I think the comparison shows how I feel about that comment.

On one hand, I appreciate the ladies who have reached out to let me know they've been there, shared how they coped, or simply to let me know I'm not alone. After our first loss, I was surprised by how many close acquaintances and family members sent me private messages saying they've been there and that I have their support. There comments were very sweet.

If you're going to make a comment, how you say it is just as important as what you say. Instead of, "It's common. You'll be fine," maybe start by saying, "I, along with many women, have been there and can understand how hard this must be for you..." Most importantly, when someone told me how common it was and that I was going to be just fine one day, that person has never experienced pregnancy loss. For them to tell me that I'll be fine and dandy, since this happens to "so many people," is wrong and upsets me still to this day when I think about it. She has absolutely no idea. Do not act like you get it and know, when you don't. One of my biggest pet Peeves is when someone tells me they know how I feel or they "feel my pain," when they've never experienced pregnancy loss.

In some cases, not all, it is beneficial to muster up the courage to confront thoughtless remarks. How else will people learn how to support you if you don't let them know that what they say could come off as insensitive? I understand that it's tricky, because you don't want to make them feel bad for what they said because they had the best intentions, but you want to give them a little insight into how their comment made you feel. Most times, remarks aren't made with malicious intent. If your mind blanks, you can't come up with anything to say, or you don't know how to react, phrases that never fail include "I love you," "I'm sorry for your loss," "I am thinking of you," "I am praying for you," "That is so hard. Do you want to talk about it?" or simply "Here's a chai latte." Some of the best friends bring Starbucks.

One comment that did give me some comfort was, "It'll get easier with time." Some can argue that time is cruel. It has the ability to punish and things can slowly eat at you over time. The truth is, time only punishes if you let it. I think time helps and dilutes pain. It eventually makes the sharp edges soften. I promise you that there will be a day when you take a glance in the mirror and think, "I haven't felt sad today, or this week." But, while you wait for that day, what do you do? Let the edges cut you, but know that they won't cut forever.

In the beginning, before I knew better, I questioned if I deserved it. Maybe, for some unknown reason, I deserved to be cut so badly by those rigid edges. What I realized, though, is that we all sin or do bad things, but no one deserves to get cut forever. Those important dates, like the babies' due dates or when we lost them, will creep up each year and I'll cry every time. The hurt never goes away completely, but I have faith that it will fade. It's safe to say my level of devastation has lessened since the days we found out about the losses. At least there's that. Grief never ends entirely, though. It just changes. There isn't a finish line that says, "Grieving ends here. It's over." Grief is a passage, not a place where you build a home to stay. Grieving is not a sign of weakness or lack of faith either. Grief and hurt means you care and you love. Those are qualities to admire, not criticize or beat yourself up over.

People you interact with often feel compelled to give you answers, to solve the problem, and that's why they have to make an excuse or thoughtless comment. It's unfortunate, because I guess all I really wanted from others throughout our pregnancy loss experience was for someone to listen, understand that what my husband and I went through is really tough, and be a friend. Heck, distract me with funny stories or binge eat some ice cream with me while we watch Disney movies. I wasn't looking for someone to give me answers, because there aren't any.

Sometimes bad things just happen. That year, I had a family member who had been battling cancer for quite some time. He was kicking its butt, but we suspected we'd have to say goodbye to him too soon because of the cancer. However, one morning I got the news that he had passed away from falling off of a ladder and hitting his head. He fought that cancer like a champion, but ended up passing away from something entirely unrelated. It goes to show that sometimes bad things just happen. I think that God takes control of circumstances sometimes, to remind us that some things are out of our control. God is using us for something greater that we may not understand now, or possibly ever.

19

DADS MOURNE TOO

Quite a few studies show that husbands or boyfriends of women who miscarry feel like they can't talk about their feelings. There are number of articles and pieces of advice for women floating around out there if you look, but hardly anything can be found to help men. I foolishly thought that I was more invested in our quest to add a branch to our family tree. I thought I wanted a baby more than my husband did and that I had even pushed the idea on him in some way. Boy, was I wrong. Those little beans meant just as much to him as they did to myself.

When we lost baby number one, I'm disappointed to admit that I was surprised that my husband shed tears, wanted to take time off work, and was devastated. I don't know how I expected him to react, but that wasn't it. He had been so quiet leading up to that awful day that I wasn't fully aware of how excited he had been. He's such a quiet person in general. I foolishly thought he didn't care as much as I did. After the first loss, my emotions were on display and raw, but I learned that he had been burying his.

I hurt for my husband. After being together for years, I should have known better than to think he didn't care as much as I did. He is guided by his heart and that's one of the reasons I love him so much. It always leads the way for him.

After our second loss, my husband's co-worker had just had a baby and she was adorable from what I could see in photos that were posted on social media. Little did my husband know, his co-worker brought the cute little girl into work the week of our loss. He texted me and I could tell it affected him more than he wanted to admit. A twinge of guilt prodded at me because he had suggested staying home from work that morning. I had shot down the idea, because I was out of paid time off at work and I thought we could get through it without wallowing around at home. Being distracted at work would be better than being alone with our thoughts. I was trying to tell myself that, anyway. Had I supported his wish to stay home, I could have saved him a little pain. I remember texting my husband back, trying to be supportive, and at the same time feeling awful. I couldn't imagine being around a baby at that point in time. Ironically, as luck would have it, about an hour after my last text to him, a woman stopped into my work with her week-old baby and I experienced the same situation my husband had been faced with. It was not pleasant and all I wanted to do was run from the room in tears. I didn't, though. No one looked at me to see my reaction, thank goodness. Why would they? The world doesn't revolve around my feelings. I sat at my desk, avoided the group of women oogling at the newborn at the front counter, and threw myself into the project I was working on.

Men are supposed to be tough. A man is supposed to be the rock of a relationship, the main source of stability, and act with void of emotion. This notion is beyond silly, but that is what culture has shoved down our throats. My husband didn't feel like he could share his feelings with me because I was broken into pieces myself and he wanted to be strong and high-spirited for me.

We women are naturally more emotional creatures. From a young age, we're taught to openly express our feelings, to be gentle and kind, whereas little boys are taught the opposite. Showing any emotion aside from anger means you are weak. So then, when little boys grow up and it comes time for them to take action and express emotion or talk about their feelings, they struggle with opening up. They don't know how. When faced with an emotionally charged situation, men sometimes fall back on the only accepted manly emotion, anger. Rather than acknowledging hurt, it's more comfortable for men to bite back and get angry about it, if they confront their feelings at all.

Maybe men think that women's heartbreak is more valid than theirs because women are the ones who physically experience everything involved with miscarriage - the symptoms, changes, and physical pain. Men gravitate toward being practical versus showing their significant other that they are grieving too.

A couple of months after our second loss I was having a terrible, no-good week. That Saturday, my husband and I decided to make our monthly trip to Sioux City, Iowa to Sam's Club and make a Walmart stop as well to stock our pantries. Sioux City is a couple of hours away and we save money by buying in bulk once a month. While shopping, we spotted the liquor aisle and down that aisle they had two sizes of one of my favorite things, RumChata. For those of you who don't know what this liquid goodness is, it's a cream liqueur that was released in 2009, made from a blend of five-time distilled Caribbean rums and Wisconsin dairy cream. It's flavored with cinnamon, vanilla, and other 'secret flavors,' so it tastes like Cinnamon Toast Crunch cereal in liquid form.

In the store, my husband and I debated for a matter of minutes about whether or not we should purchase the $35.00 bottle. Ultimately, my husband told me to toss it in the cart. Life is short, drink the Cinnamon Toast Crunch goodness. I was so excited! Of all the things we bought that day, it was one of the purchases I was most looking forward to.

When we got home, I told my husband that I should let the dog out to go potty quickly first, and then I'd come back and we could unload. He was rather impatient. That, and I think he was trying to be kind and get a head start at unloading so that I wouldn't have to do as much. In any case, when I came back in from walking the dog, he trudged in from the garage at the same time and looked at me with sad eyes saying, "I'm sorry." I said, "Sorry for what?" "I made a mistake," he said. Irritated, I replied, "Spit it out, what is wrong?!" He told me that he had grabbed the plastic Walmart bag and it tore from the weight of the liquor bottle. The bottle of RumChata fell to the driveway, shattered, and the cement was drowning in our white rum deliciousness.

There I was, angry about wasted money, angry there was no RumChata for that evening, and upset my husband had tracked in sticky goo on my newly mopped kitchen floor. I'm embarrassed to admit I don't mop the floors often and I had just mopped the floor the day before. This whole incident was no big deal, right? People make mistakes and it was only a broken bottle. It was more than that, though. Leading up to that moment, I had already been upset with him for several reasons. Navigating through the aftermath of pregnancy loss puts a strain on a couple's relationship, no matter how perfect you are for each other. Emotions run high and things that weren't stressful before become a bit complicated. Being the poor communicator that I can tend to be, I hadn't voiced much of my feelings. That week had been the due date for baby number one and my husband hadn't acknowledged it. On the due date, I knew he didn't remember what day it was because guys are notoriously bad at remembering those sorts of things, I had reminded him. All he said was, "yeah." What?! All he said was, "yeah!"

Our babies are never talked about. As a matter of fact, my husband never talks about much of anything. He's not a talker. That's not necessarily a bad trait. It's just how he is. From what I could see, he was never sad about what happened with our losses. The breaking of the RumChata bottle was the straw that broke the camel's back for me. Silly, but accurate. I tried to remain calm and not irrationally yell at him for making a simple mistake. I knew he wouldn't understand that I was mad at him for far more than breaking a bottle of liquor. However, it escalated to a huge fight. We were both screaming and crying, and I let him know that I was mad that he never talks to me about our babies or wanting to try again. I was mad that it seemed so easy for him to deal with our losses, when I felt like I was barely keeping my head above water. We had both been slacking in the area of communication. So, we fought, yelled, cried, and put everything out on the table. It was refreshing. I had screamed at him that he never acknowledges that anything happened, as if he was unfazed. He proceeded to yell back at me, "Do you think I'm not hurt?! I don't know how to talk to you. I don't talk. I don't share things. Teach me how. Tell me what I'm supposed to do. I want more than anything to be a dad, and I could have been right now. Do you think I don't know that?!" That broke my heart. That was the most he'd ever said about any of it. Pregnancy loss has the potential to have a very damaging effect on marriages. My husband and I were both suffering, yet in being too busy focusing on our own feelings, we missed recognizing each other's need for support. We secretly blamed each other for not meeting our respective needs. I expected my husband to know or read my mind to find out what I needed from him.

From that point on, we devised a plan to talk to each other more. I didn't realize he had been struggling with figuring out how to talk about our losses. I'm a talker and voicing how I feel doesn't tend to be too difficult for me.

It hadn't occurred to me that my husband didn't know how to talk about his feelings.

Unconsciously, friends and family aid in making it difficult for men to open up after pregnancy loss. Up until a loss, the joy is most often a joint experience for both mom and dad. Congratulations are given to both sides of the couple. When a baby is lost though, the spotlight is shown only on the woman, illuminating and bringing to the forefront how only she feels, and how she's coping. Men feel invisible and insignificant, but they hate to admit it. I think the reason people tend to show more sympathy toward a woman is because the mom is pregnant, and they see miscarriage and pregnancy loss as one in the same. Those people are wrong. Miscarriage and pregnancy loss are different in the sense that the mom may suffer through the actual miscarriage, but both parents suffer a loss. The only ones who think to ask how the grieving dad is doing are either his mother or other men who are floating in the same boat - other men who have experienced the devastation of pregnancy loss. Men have just as much right to grieve as women, because lost babies are just as much a loss to them as to the women.

If you and your significant other help make up the twenty five percent who have been affected by miscarriage, from the bottom of my heart, my sympathy goes to both mommy and daddy. As you continue to cope with your loss and search for some peace, please don't believe the myth that men aren't emotionally capable of mourning, or that they'll refuse support or sympathy. It disappoints me to think about how I acted before I opened my eyes a little and it saddens me that people don't give dads of miscarried babies the sympathy they deserve. So, ladies who have lost, give your partner a little more credit because he is also grieving.

20

Following Up

After our losses, I thought that what I needed was answers. If I knew why this was happening, it would make it better or easier to swallow. In my story, that wasn't the case. At one of my first pregnancy appointments with the second doctor I saw, I voiced my fear of multiple miscarriages, of tragedy striking a second time. He told me that if my second pregnancy ended in miscarriage (which it did), they wouldn't look into why my miscarriages were happening until I had three or more. The reason for this is because most women who have one or two miscarriages will go on to have a successful pregnancy. When that happens, it suggests that their first or second miscarriage was a fluke instead of in result of an underlying cause. After my first miscarriage, my doctor told me that bodies try to correct themselves after miscarriages and the same exact complication that ended the first pregnancy rarely causes additional miscarriages. If additional miscarriages occur, it will be because of something else. In any case, the theory about three consecutive miscarriages was established in the 1930's without many facts to support it. The three-miscarriage-rule has since been scrapped, but most doctors still believe it and use the rule.

When my second miscarriage happened, I was sad on top of everything else because I didn't think anyone would do anything to help. I knew I'd have to go through something like that again at least one more time before I could get help, or there simply wasn't anything anyone could do to help. However, my nurse ended up calling me, saying the doctor did recommend I see a specialist. I was in luck! Or so I thought. I expected to get all these tests run and one of those would magically tell me why my body couldn't keep a baby alive.

The specialist told me about tests that were available. I swear he listed off eight to ten, and that was just scraping the surface of possibilities. Who knew there were so many reasons why miscarriages occur? Tests that could be done, to name a handful, include hormonal factors tests, structural factors tests, tests to examine my uterine lining, chromosomal testing, and blood tests to check my immune system. Issues with any one of those could be the cause of our losses. One could write a pretty thick, extensive book on tests that can be done, but I won't delve much deeper, because that's not my aim for this book. Trust me that the testing options are virtually innumerable.

After the specialist told me about the tests he could run, he said that if I wanted to proceed, the best test to start with in my situation would be the chromosomal testing. Then, he proceeded to let me know that it would cost around one thousand dollars per person, as both my husband and I would need the test. It wouldn't be covered under insurance. We aren't poor, but my husband and I aren't necessarily swimming in pools of money. No matter how desperately we want children, two thousand dollars or more at that moment, for only one of the tests with no guarantee of answers, was not something that seemed practical, much less something we could really afford. Even if we do run every test possible and spend thousands of dollars someday, we could still end up with no answers and no better chance of having a rainbow baby in the future. I've read that about half of the couples who have investigated their miscarriages don't come out with any clear answers. Not getting answers is obviously frustrating, but it is also good news because that means that there is a good chance of the next pregnancy being viable and healthy, without any treatment necessary at all. If we do tests and find some sort of answer, there aren't preventative measures we can take to avoid future miscarriages. The answers we'd find would just be another thing to hover over us.

My husband and I decided that we were going to put everything in God's hands. I was exhausted with going to doctor offices and thinking about what to do next. I was emotionally overwhelmed with the whole ordeal. When we decided that, I was still recovering from the second pregnancy loss, so I was cranky and it was a lot to handle.

During period weeks, I use tampons and have for as long as I can remember. After the second miscarriage, I needed to wear pads instead and it didn't go well. I got a rash from where the pads rubbed and then I found out I was allergic to something in the brand of pads I had purchased. I ended up getting a rash everywhere in the nether region as a result. It was rash city down there, and that fueled my anger, frustration, and sadness. So, almost needless to say, at that point I was done. Done with it all. Visualize a little girl in a store that just got told no when she asked for a brand new toy. After throwing a fit, she sits down on the ground and pouts. That was pretty much my attitude. That is probably how I looked in our restroom that day, sitting on the floor throwing a childish fit by myself. Ridiculous, but accurate.

My husband and I decided that we were going to heal from our losses and take life one day at a time. We'd find joy in other places while we waited. We were going to try our hardest to focus on other things. My focus was getting back in shape, lose some pesky weight, and possibly train for another marathon. If we are meant to be parents, we will be one day. God is just taking extra time to make us the most wonderful baby.

21

THE PREGNANT LADY
I WANT TO BE

This experience is still going on for me. I'll never forget our losses, so I imagine it will be a never-ending experience. My losses were months ago, but at times it's still fresh and I'm still in the stages of grieving. One thing I've learned throughout all of this is to be courteous and careful of what you say when there are others around. This applies to life in general. Always be thoughtful and kind. More specifically applying to my story, when I talk about babies or children now, I'm more careful of who is around me and what I say, because I know how it feels to be struggling while being subjected to baby conversation.

It's simple – think before you complain, whether that's in person or on social media. You're privy to your opinions and thoughts, and you're encouraged to voice them, but you never know who is listening or reading.

If you're a good person, you don't want to intentionally hurt anyone. Be thoughtful of what others might be going through, their hidden battles. I can barely tolerate when women vent about how they're tired of being pregnant or complain about pregnancy symptoms.

Yes, I understand that your social media page is just that - it's yours. You have every right to vent about feeling miserable. It's your outlet for self-expression. If I don't like it, I don't have to read it. Keep scrolling. I get that. I also realize that just because you are venting about feeling terrible, doesn't mean you aren't thankful for the gift with which you've been blessed. However, it hurts women like me to see stuff like that, because I'd give anything to be suffering through your symptoms. I'm actually jealous of your miserable symptoms or lack of sleep! Count yourself lucky and if you want to complain, text or call a close friend or family member you trust. I'm truly sorry you don't feel well or your children are making you want to rip your hair out, but maybe take a second to think about those of us who would love to be in your shoes before you make a complaining public post for all to see or vent to a group of co-workers in the break room of your work place.

If the time comes when I'm blessed with a healthy pregnancy, I know just the kind of pregnant lady I will strive to be. I won't flaunt it like some women. There is a huge difference between being happy about becoming a mother (being excited and sharing things with your friends), and rubbing it in people's faces or being obnoxious about it. I guess it's not those obnoxious gals' fault for acting that way, because unless you've suffered a loss, you probably don't think about who is listening or reading before you rant about your pregnancy.

Gushing about all the gifts you've received and how spoiled your little one is already, gloating about how wonderful your pregnant life is, or constantly rubbing your belly to draw attention to it are all things that irritate the crap out of me. It bothered me more back then because I was grieving and extra sensitive. It doesn't bother me as much anymore, but the point is we get it. You're pregnant. Can you and I interact without your pregnancy being the center of attention all of the time? Can we find a balance between obsessing over the fact that you have a baby in your belly and ignoring it? Can we just acknowledge that your pregnant, but still focus on other things, please?

Since I've been through miscarriages now, if that time comes for my husband and I, I will strive to be thoughtful. You never know what someone you're talking to is going through, whether that be infertility issues or struggling with moving past loss(es).

22

FAMOUS WOMEN WHO HAVE LOST

I look up to celebrities and place a few of them on a pedestal so high that it could reach the clouds, thinking that they're untouchable. I'm not alone in acting this way. That way of thinking is why those individuals are celebrities. They have extensive followers and large fan bases that maintain their social status. Well, bad things happen to celebrities too. They aren't exempt from human trials. The media paints pretty pictures of their lives with interview after article after post of happy marriages, beautiful trips around the world, and baby bumps. But, when a celebrity suffers pregnancy loss, like many of us they often keep it a secret in order to preserve their perfect image that they've worked so hard to build. Pregnancy losses only seem to surface after a celebrity is pregnant with a new healthy baby or after a fresh accomplishment in their life has surfaced. That is why coming forward and speaking up about pregnancy loss has been a scarce occurrence until somewhat recently. Within the last few years, giving comfort and providing support for other families has trumped any fear of embarrassment or inadequacy by celebrities. There seems to be a new movement that focuses on support and comfort. I love the direction in which we're headed, toward being more open, accepting, and supportive of each other through loss.

Every Sunday, my church takes a few minutes to open up the service to anyone in the room to express prayer requests or to acknowledge deaths and illnesses. People raise their hands and announce deaths, upcoming surgeries, or deployments and ask for the church members' prayers and good vibes. No one in their right mind would raise their hand to acknowledge a miscarriage, or at least that is how I feel. Everyone else, if they're comfortable, can share their loss or pain, but pregnancy loss survivors (yes, that's what we are - survivors) don't have that same opportunity. The benefit of being in the celebrity spotlight is that there is always an audience willing to listen. Responses may not always be positive, but in the case of pregnancy loss, having an audience is a really great thing. Most of we "normal" women without celebrity status don't have a dedicated audience or an open, accepting space like that to navigate through our loss. In our non-celebrity world, funerals help us heal from death and illnesses are prayed for, but there are no maps to direct us down the road of pregnancy loss.

Having said that, I respect and support the celebrities of late who have had the courage to publicize their struggles in order to stop the secrecy and countermand the stigma about miscarriage. It takes immense courage to divulge anything personal about yourself, and pregnancy loss is a big one. The more celebrities (those who have a louder voice and can reach more people) who share their heartache, the more steps toward open acknowledgement of the frequency of and pain that comes with pregnancy loss.

Lisa Ling, an author and journalist whom I remember primarily from hosting *The View* from 1999-2002, started her own website called the "Secret Society of Women," hoping to create an online community for women to seek support. Women can share their feelings and tell their story. In 2010, Lisa announced that she had suffered a miscarriage earlier in the year. "We actually [hadn't] been trying that long," she said on one episodes of *The View* [14]. "I don't know that I took it as seriously as I should have because [the pregnancy] happened so fast. But then when I heard the doctor say there was no heartbeat it was like—bam—like a knife through the heart" [14]. She was about two months along when she lost her baby. The experience left her feeling like an utter failure and terrified of miscarrying again in the future, feelings we miscarriage mamas can relate to wholeheartedly. Three years later, Lisa gave birth to a daughter and then had a second daughter in 2016.

Actress and Broadway performer Ashley Williams wrote a boldly honest blog post a few months after her miscarriage. The star I recognize from her role as Victoria on *How I Met Your Mother* shared how shocked she was to learn about the widespread nature of miscarriage. I couldn't relate more to Williams when she wrote, "If 25 percent of my peers are currently experiencing miscarriages right alongside me, why wasn't I prepared? Why don't we talk about it? Why was I feeling embarrassed, broken, like a walking wound?" [15]. Ashley also wrote, "Not many people talk about a pregnancy until 12 weeks gestation for fear they will lose the baby or choose to terminate for any number of complex reasons. What's the point in telling people who never knew you were pregnant the depressing news that you're not anymore? My (still bloated) gut feeling is that something even more painful silences us—the fear that we, as women, are failures" [15]. Williams pushes for women to speak up about miscarriages, writing, "I invite you to start, with me, a vocal army of the 25 percenters who can normalize miscarriage in the social sphere. You are not broken. You did nothing wrong. You are strong, you are brave, and there is hope" [15] I can't expand on her words, because she phrased her thoughts so perfectly. Each time I read Williams' words, I tear up, because it's so relieving to know someone else understands and, even if I've never met Ashley Williams, she's on my side.

In 2012, Nicole Kidman spoke about her fertility troubles saying, "I had tried and failed and failed and failed. Not to be too detailed, but I've had an ectopic pregnancy, miscarriages and I've had fertility treatments. I've done all the stuff you can possibly do to try get pregnant" [10]. After pregnancy loss, we can feel so useless and broken. It's important to have hope and faith in your dreams.

Today, the actress is mom to one daughter whom she gave birth to, two children she adopted, and one daughter who was born via surrogate. Nicole is a great example of a mom who never gave up, despite feeling inadequate and in spite of every door that seemed to be slammed in her face. She makes me want to never give up.

A couple of days after Beyoncé´ gave birth to Blue Ivy, her husband Jay-Z released a rap that reveals their miscarriage heartache. His lyrics include, "Last time the miscarriage was so tragic / We was afraid you'd disappear / But nah baby, you magic" [6]. Beyoncé said, "About two years ago, I was pregnant for the first time and I heard the heartbeat, which was the most beautiful music I ever heard in my life" [8]. The couple had picked out names and their dreams were becoming reality. Instead, when Beyoncé flew to New York for a checkup, the heartbeat wasn't there. The news flipped her world upside down. Just the week prior, she had been to the doctor and everything had been fine. She said that after the devastating appointment, she went into the studio and wrote the saddest song she had ever written in her life, called <u>Heartbeat</u>. That song was her therapy. Again, being able to relate to someone is such a comfort. I've felt similar pain. Beyoncé's comfort was writing music and some of my comfort came from writing this book.

In 2014, *Duck Dynasty* stars Jase and Missy Robertson told the world about their loss that happened in 2002. It took them twelve years to muster the courage or find the necessity to publicize it, but they did, and that is so powerful. Missy shared, "I was about eight to ten weeks along when I miscarried, just enough time to be excited about it and start telling everyone" [2]. Missy had been worried that she might not be able to have more children after their loss, but she and Jase had another daughter a few months later. I can relate to Missy's story in the sense that I'm concerned about whether or not I'll ever be able to have children. Seeing her strength and ultimate happy ending gives me hope.

Lily Allen is one of my favorite vocalists. She has experienced both a miscarriage in 2008 and stillbirth at six months pregnant in 2010. The singer explains that even though what she has been through is completely devastating, it made her see what she has and appreciate it, something she never did before. Lily has been pretty straight forward about her miscarriage. Feeling heartbroken she said, "It was horrendous and something I would not wish on my worst enemy. It's something that I still haven't dealt with. I never will get over it. I have dealt with it, you know, as being at one with it. But it's not something that you get over. I held my child and it was really horrific and painful — one of the hardest things that can happen to a person" [7] You never get over something like that. You move forward and learn how to live life knowing you have a baby in Heaven. By God's grace, Lily and her husband Sam Cooper are now parents to two girls. Lily says that it's awful that her husband and she had to experience those horrendous things, but through it they became closer. I can relate to that. My husband and I are closer than ever. There's always a silver lining if you look for it.

It took Lady Antebellum singer Hillary Scott nearly a year to feel comfortable with speaking publicly about her miscarriage. She told *Good Morning America*, "This is something that is still not talked about very often. I also feel like there's this pressure that you're just supposed to be able to snap your fingers, and continue to walk through life like it never happened" [9]. Hillary has talked about how having a miscarriage has given her a new perspective on life and she's almost a whole different mom to her two-year-old as a result, a more nurturing and thankful mom who smothers her little girl with love every chance she can get. She is a mother figure to look up to, that's for sure. She doesn't take any small moments for granted. Knowing that, you can find some light in the darkness that is pregnancy loss. Along with Lily Allen, Hillary found solace in music.

Famous singer, Tori Amos, opened up to *Now magazine* and Channel 4 News in her area about her three miscarriages that occurred before she was blessed with her rainbow baby. Many of we pregnancy loss survivors can relate to her words, "Going through this horror, I was humbled by what it was to be a woman," she said [1]. "I could be a female icon and successful breadwinner, but my body couldn't carry a child" [1]. We can be the most beautiful and accomplished human beings in existence, but when we can't seem to have a healthy baby or get pregnant, we are distraught and crippled with the thought that we are inadequate, useless, or a complete and utter failure.

I've noticed that some women portray a somewhat nonchalant way of dealing with pregnancy loss, which I find interesting to examine. Maybe it's just a cover, or maybe it's legitimate. Who knows? In 2009, singer

Céline Dion spoke with *Access Hollywood* about trying to have a second child with husband Rene Angelil. Celine said she had known she was pregnant for a few days, but somewhat coldly commented that "it didn't stay" [4]. In an interview with Oprah, Celine was optimistic, saying, "Its life, you know? A lot of people go through this. We tried four times to have a child. We're still trying. We're on the fifth try, and I'll tell you, if five is my lucky number, this fifth try has got to come in" [5]. She and her husband struggled with infertility for years and did several rounds of IVF. Not only in the professional world, but in her personal life as well, Celine is a shimmering example of not giving up on your dreams and not letting life get you down.

Actually, I could go on for pages and pages about famous women who have come forward to speak publically about their pregnancy loss experience, but I'll mention one more. A quote by Christie Brinkley, a famous American model and actress, sums up my feelings like hitting a nail right on the head. In a 1998 interview with *Good Housekeeping*, she spoke openly about having three miscarriages. "After the first miscarriage, I tried to take the attitude that it was my body's way of telling me that this pregnancy wasn't meant to be, and that it was better for everybody," she said. "But after the second one, it was really devastating. Four months is a lot of living with that little life in you — thinking about it, eating right for it, nurturing it and all of a sudden, it dies" [11] Yes. Just yes. Some may try to minify your feelings because your child never lived outside of the womb, but you spent days, weeks, or months housing that little baby, feeding it, and helping it live. It's a life-changer when that baby you have been responsible for dies, for no reason in most cases.

About one in one hundred couples experience multiple miscarriages (three or more). I can tell you, too, that having multiple miscarriages and having the experience of one under your belt so-to-speak does not make the next one less traumatic. After my first miscarriage, I had this mindset that this horrible disaster was out of our way. I experienced it and it won't happen again. So, the next time I was pregnant, I didn't realistically think miscarriage would happen multiple times. It's a difficult feeling to try to explain. On one hand I didn't think tragedy would strike again, but on the other hand I was nervous about everything as a result of the first miscarriage. The second miscarriage was just as heartbreaking as the first.

Several celebrities, including Marilyn Monroe, have had repeat miscarriages. Olympic skater Nancy Kerrigan had six miscarriages in an eight year time period between her first and second child. It's a tricky and very personal decision to make - do you try again right away after a miscarriage, or do you give yourself time to heal emotionally? Doctors will recommend fully healing both physically and mentally. My doctors recommended waiting six months before trying again after each loss, but I tended to ignore that advice both times. There has been research that dabbles with the idea that women who try to get pregnant again soon after miscarriage might be more successful than those who take some time before trying again. I've heard that you're more fertile after a miscarriage, and especially after a D&C procedure, as your system is "cleaned out" and "fresh," to put it in very blunt and insensitive terms. I'm not sure there are hard facts to back that theory, though. The theory rang true after my first miscarriage, anyway.

Nearly all celebrity parents who've experienced miscarriage or loss that the public knows of have ended up welcoming children into their lives through one method or another. Some, like Celine Dion and Brooke Shields took the IVF route and had healthy babies. Others, like Barbara Walters and Sharon Stone chose to adopt. A few, like Nicole Kidman and Giuliana Rancic, opted for surrogacy. Never give up on your dreams, even when they seem impossible. If you know in your heart that you're meant to be a mom, there are options. Surrogacy or adoption may not be your first choice when it comes to having kids, but just because you've had pregnancy troubles doesn't mean God doesn't want you to be a mom. Try to be open to the different plans He may have in store for you.

23

WITHOUT THE RAIN, THERE WOULD BE NO RAINBOW

Now, most days I have an optimistic outlook on my husband and I's situation, but it took a long time to reach that point. I was devastated, mad, and consumed with feeling sorry for myself for a long time. Heck, I still have those days, but I'm happy to say that they are few in number. I can tell you about the day that my outlook changed.

I had gotten to the point where I wasn't very active, eating my feelings and slowly gaining more weight. I was more depressed than I'd ever been and I weighed the most I had ever weighed. Unfortunately, unhealthy food had been one source of comfort for a while. Many of my friends had just had babies or were pregnant, and I was there missing what we had lost. Overall, I felt like I had hit rock bottom. It's almost too personal to admit, but some days my depression got so bad that I contemplated why I was even alive. I wondered if the world would be better off without me. Maybe the pain would go away if I wasn't here any longer. At one point, dramatic Nikki thought, *I can't manage to have babies, so what's my purpose?* That was my lowest point, but thankfully I eventually snapped out of it. Suicide may take away your pain in the moment, but it takes your pain and transfers it to the people you love the most. It's just a bad chapter in your book of life, not a bad life. There is help if you get to a point where you start wondering if suicide is an option. Please refer to chapter twenty six and know that you are loved. You do have a purpose.

The morning my attitude started to change, I was on my way to work. I had just downloaded some new music, so I was consumed by my speakers, singing away and snacking on chocolate chip Teddy Grahams. Yes, it's acceptable for adults to eat those too! We had a fairly new car. At that point it was going on two years old. Sometimes I still learn new things while driving Kody (that's what we named it, because its color according to the factory was Kodiak brown). I live in a town of about four hundred, so the roads are usually pretty clear. I rarely meet another car on my commute in the morning. There is a lot of wide open space, taken up by either fields or pasture. In any case, it was a crisp forty degree morning and I apparently hadn't gotten the grasp of how to work the defrost yet. It was early, so it was still fairly dark. I was halfway there and for some reason the defrost acted up and my entire windshield went opaque instantly. I couldn't see and adrenaline started to rush. Reflex kicked in and

I turned my wipers on, just in time to clear my view and see a deer pop out in front of my vehicle. I braked hard and missed hitting it by mere inches. It had to have been a matter of inches because I swear I felt the whoosh of the deer as I missed it. Heck, maybe I even grazed its fur, but I'll stop being overly dramatic. I know I wouldn't have died or even been severely injured had I ended up hitting the deer, but I knew that God was watching over me that morning.

Not having to deal with a wrecked car at that point in my life was truly a blessing. We needed to pay medical bills, not a car repair bill. An event that was fairly small got my mind reeling about how foolish I had been acting. Yes, our losses were awful and life-changing, but I have so much to be grateful for. It was a bad chapter in my book, not a bad life. There's no lemon so sour that you can't make something resembling lemonade. Anymore, when I have those days where I'm acting foolishly like a brat, thinking that life is so awful and things can't get much worse, I take two fingers and find my pulse. There it is. That is something to be grateful for, another day breathing on this beautiful planet.

In times of loneliness and heartache, I had prayed for God to bring me a kind, compassionate, and patient man. He did. Heck, I prayed for so many things over the years that God so graciously granted. It's funny how when something bad happens, we magically forget all the good God has done for us. The day I quit feeling so sorry for myself every chance I got, I realized that all of us often take for granted what others are praying for. I have a roof over my head, job, and vehicle. I adore my family, have a couple of friends who would do anything for me, and am married to the most incredible man. Those blessings are what my lemonade consists of and somehow, all of that had shifted to the backburner.

My husband and I have always been extremely close, almost to the point of being creepy how compatible we are. Throughout the last year or so, we've grown even closer. Sure, there were a couple of bumps, but he has officially seen me at my worst and loves me more for it. How many people can say they have that kind of person in their lives; Someone who doesn't back down or run away when the going gets tough, but steps up and possesses an impressive optimistic outlook on life?

Once a good amount of time passed, I saw that my resentment and bitterness toward God was my entire fault. All along I was looking for somewhere to point my finger and aim my anger. I was desperate for someone else to blame and I had chosen God. I was wrong. I had all of these unattainable expectations for Him. I acted like such a spoiled brat, being so entitled. I thought I deserved all of the things that I wanted, but boy was I mistaken. Not one time in the Bible does God promise that if we are good, He will grant all of our desires. Him and I, we never made that deal. Yet, that's what most of us Christians often think, right? If I'm a good girl, I'll get what I want. So many falsely believe that God is like Santa. He watches us all year long and if we are good, we'll be rewarded with gifts. Funny enough, not only does God never promise us that, but the Bible actually tells us the opposite. It clearly says that none of us are good. Everyone sins and we do it over and over and over again. Yet, God still loves us and is our steadfast teacher.

Each time my husband and I lost a baby, I'd ask myself *Why would my perfect and amazing God let this happen? Life isn't fair! Doesn't God love everyone the same? Why can so-and-so have such a beautiful life, but we can't have a child?* All of the deals that I assumed had been made between myself and God were figments of my imagination. They were made up. Many of us live with this false idea that if we do something "good" for God, he is obligated to return the favor - he just has to. When He doesn't follow through exactly how we want, we are furious and frustrated. We are His children and we certainly act like just that - children - sometimes. Those actions are a result of our crazy false expectations. The Bible describes how we aren't good and, like life in general, unconditional love isn't always fair. God spent time on and crafted each of us and loved us with every ounce of His being, just for us to turn around and disappoint him, letting him down time after time. If we ever think we're getting jipped out of something we feel like we deserve, how do you think God feels? Despite all of our sins, He continues to love us, no matter what we do. How beautiful. I want to bring up that so many individuals we read about in the Bible, people Jesus admired, suffered unimaginable devastation, yet kept their faith. Even the purest, good people were tested. Yes, a few questioned their faith, but they were ultimately always faithful and true. If extraordinary figures like that were hit with misfortune, why would someone like me be worthy of a life without adversity. I'm not. Everyone will be touched with some sort of hardship at some point. That's life.

I hope someday my husband and I will hold a rainbow baby in our arms. Without a soggy and uncomfortable downpour, there is no chance for a beautiful rainbow in the end. My husband and I will appreciate the gift of a baby more than we ever would have before. When we get exhausted, weak, or struggle in any way while caring for our child(ren), we will think before we speak a word of complaint or disdain. As Charles Dickens in *Great Expectations* so perfectly puts it, "I have been bent and broken, but - I hope - into a better shape" [3] Throughout our heartbreaks, I haven't been completely broken, just molded into a better shape. I keep telling myself to let my past make me better, not bitter. When life shuts a door, open it again. It's a door. That's how they work.

When we are hurt and can't manage to figure out why we are going through what we are facing, it's hard to have hope or trust in God. I've questioned Him more times than I care to admit. Something that helped me was the idea that God is simply a good Father. Although I can't tell you first hand, I know that being a parent isn't always about being the "good" guy. There were plenty of times throughout my childhood that I disliked my mom and dad. Sometimes mommies and daddies have to be the "bad" guy for their child's benefit. Parents put their kids in time-out to teach them not to stick kitchen utensils in or around the electrical outlets, take them to the doctor for their yearly unpleasant shots to stay healthy, or make them do chores to instill good work ethic at a young age. Parents do these things and become the big bad meanie butt in their children's' eyes. Kids usually don't realize it at the time, but everything their parents do is for their own good and is done with the best intentions. When we are faced with trials, look at those situations with the knowledge that God is trying to be the best father that he can. He understands the pain we feel, because He feels it with us. God knows our heart and He would never give our heart desires He would not deliver with. He knows just how much each of us can handle and trials happen because He has a beautiful plan for each of us.

I look at everything so differently several months post loss. One thing I know for sure is that had I known sooner about the struggles that my parents went through to bring me into the world, I wouldn't have been such a brat growing up, or at least I would have made more of an effort to be less brat-like. The truth is, if you truly realized how much your parents loved you from the very moment they saw a positive pregnancy test, how badly your parents wanted you, or what they went through to bring you into the world, I bet you'd regret being such a little shit when you were younger. I do. You'd regret those times you threw a tantrum because you didn't get your way and you'd be disappointed in yourself for all those times you said you'd rather be anywhere else but around them. Why? The chances are that they wanted you more than you'll ever know. They dreamed, prayed, and hoped for you. I remember I was so mad at my mom one time, that I told her I wished my aunt Val was my mom instead of her. Even though I was pretty little, I'll never forget my mom's face when I said that and how she cried. I can't imagine the pain she must have felt - wanting a child so badly and bringing one in the world, just to have that child turn around and reject her, even if the comments were made without thought and were the backlash of anger. Now that I've tried to start a family of my own for some time and lost babies in the process, I have a new appreciation for the struggles my own parents went through. They prayed, worried, fought, and lost sleep all for me. I am forever grateful.

I can picture myself holding a sweet baby, sniffing the top of his or her head, watching them wrap their tiny fingers around my behemoth of an index finger, knowing that my only job in the world is to protect them. In that moment, I'll love my parents even more.

A nationally recognized author, Cheryl Strayed once cleverly wrote in her book *Tiny Beautiful Things: Advice on Love and Life from Dear Sugar,* "You don't have a right to the cards you believe you should have been dealt. You have an obligation to play the hell out of the one you're holding" [12]. I've read few things more true than that statement. We don't have a right to a perfect life and we aren't exempt from human suffering. We have a responsibility to live the life we are given to its fullest. Again, there is no lemon so sour that you can't make something resembling lemonade. I no longer think that trials are a curse. They're more of a second (or third or fourth or...) chance. They are an invitation to better ourselves and get to know God on a different level. Sometimes, we are taken into troubled waters not to drown, but to be cleansed.

As I write the last sections of this book, my story is still unfinished, but that's okay. Heck, by the time my words are actually printed, maybe I'll be pregnant again.

Only He knows what the future holds. I don't need to have my story resolved or have a happy ending in order to share what I've been through. God uses our stories, no matter what chapter we're on, to heal others. I want so much to be able to help others heal. If this book reaches only one person and helps them in some small way, I'll consider it a success. Our stories don't need to be polished and placed in a shiny gift bag ready for delivery before God can use them. I wish my story ended with "What I told you was all pretty unfortunate, but now we have three healthy children and life ended up being just the way I always pictured," but that isn't a story that God can use.

I learned something really neat the other day. In Japan, broken objects are often repaired with gold. In most areas of the world, people prefer damages to items be repaired and look brand new, without a trace of its broken history. However, the Japanese art of Kintsugi follows a different philosophy. "Kintsugi restores the broken item incorporating the damage into the aesthetic of the restored item, making it part of the object's history. Kintsugi uses lacquer resin mixed with powdered gold, silver, platinum, copper or bronze, resulting into something more beautiful than the original" [13]. The flaw is seen as a unique piece of the object's history, which adds to its beauty. Consider that when you're feeling broken. Your broken pieces make you special. When you're broken, you often come out in the end stronger and as a better version of yourself. Think about this: you can't use an egg until it is broken.

Throughout my husband and I's pregnancy losses, I haven't been the ideal model of a good Christian. I've struggled immensely. I've been mad at God and questioned my beliefs, but I've come to realize that God is always good. It may have been a bumpy road there for a bit, but I ended up where I needed to be - one hundred percent in love with God. His worthiness or greatness doesn't depend on whether or not my prayers are answered to the fullest. Even though my husband and I haven't been blessed with our rainbow baby quite yet, I have faith that there is hope after pregnancy loss. There is hope after an unanswered prayer. There is a rainbow after the storm. If you have ever lost anything or anyone important to you, I pray you find the same hope that I've found. With His guidance, I made it through some of the toughest days I've encountered in my life so far, and I thank Him for that. He never left me. Setting aside all of my sadness, I still have so much to be thankful for. My heart still aches for the babies we lost, but it makes me feel a little better knowing that they are safely guarded in His arms. I was like a surrogate for Heaven. God and I, we are sharing two little angels now.

24

FINAL NOTE

During my pregnancies, I periodically journaled short notes and scribbles to remember details. I began compiling those ramblings, adding to them, and writing this book about two months after our second loss. It was quite the journey. I have racked my brain over the best way to put my feelings to paper, giggled, and cried during the writing of this book. I'm so proud and happy that I get the chance to share it with you.

The morning that I submitted this book to my publishing advisor, I took a pregnancy test and found out that I am pregnant for the third time. There is a chance that this little bean won't stick, but what I've learned is that God is good and this little baby deserves for me to give it all of the love I have and cherish every moment. Hopefully, our little rainbow will be in our arms in nine months. Details about how that progresses and turns out might be material for another book, though. Thank you for your time, understanding, and open-mindedness. God bless you.

25

COMFORTING VERSES AND SONGS

Top Ten Favorite Passages of Scripture That Comfort Me:

- Isaiah 43:1 "But now, this is what the Lord says – he who created you, Jacob, he who formed you, Israel: 'Do not fear, for I have redeemed you; I have summoned you by name; you are mine.'"
  - I really love most of Isaiah, but this verse is special to me. It's the verse that is inscribed on the marble of the stone at the plot where my first baby's remains lie. These words give solace to many.
- Luke 22:42 "Father, if you are willing, take this cup from me; yet not my will, but yours be done."
- Psalm 34:17-18 "The righteous cry out, and the Lord hears them; he delivers them from all their

troubles. The Lord is close to the brokenhearted and saves those who are crushed in spirit."

- James 1:2-4 "Consider it pure joy, my brothers and sisters, whenever you face trials of many kinds, because you know that the testing of your faith produces perseverance. Let perseverance finish its work so that you may be mature and complete, not lacking anything."
- Psalm 61:2 "From the ends of the Earth I call to you, I call as my heart grows faint; lead me to the rock that is higher than I."
- John 13:7 "Jesus replied, 'You do not realize now what I am doing, but later you will understand.'"
- Jeremiah 17:7-8 "But blessed is the one who trust in the Lord, whose confidence is in Him. They will be like a tree planted by the water that sends out its roots by the stream. It does not fear when heat comes; its leaves are always green. It has no worries in a year of drought and never fails to bear fruit."
- 2 Corinthians 12:9 "But he said to me, 'My grace is sufficient for you, for my power is made perfect in weakness.'"
- Lamentations 3:25-26 "The Lord is good to those whose hope is in him, to the one who seeks him; it is good to wait quietly for the salvation of the Lord."
  - God is good to those who passionately wait, to those who diligently seek. It's okay to quietly hope for help from God. Lamentations was written by the prophet Jeremiah, often referred to as the "weeping prophet." He's

someone to listen to if we want to know how to make lemonade out of lemons. Focus on the faithfulness and steadfastness of God. He will never let you down.

- Proverbs 16:1 "To humans belong the plans of the heart, but from the Lord comes the proper answer of the tongue."

Twenty Uplifting Songs that Help Process Loss:

1. "I Would Die For That" by Kellie Coffey
2. "Beam Me Up" by Pink
3. "Thy Will" by Hilary Scott
4. "Falling Awake" by Gary Jules
5. "Slipped Away" by Avril Lavigne
6. "Heaven" by Beyoncé
7. "Glory Baby" by Watermark
8. "Small Bump" by Ed Sheeran
9. "Ten" by Yellowcard
10. "Hear You Me" by Jimmy Eat World
11. "Talking to the Moon" by Bruno Mars
12. "Tears in Heaven" by Eric Clapton
13. "I Would've Loved You Anyway" by Trisha Yearwood
14. "I Will Not Say Goodbye" by Danny Gokey
15. "There You'll Be" by Faith Hill
16. "Something's Not Right" by Lily Allen
17. "Broken" by Lifehouse
18. "To Where You Are" by Josh Groban
19. "Gone Too Soon" by Daughtry
20. "Take My Place" by Lily Allen

26

HELPFUL RESOURCES

<u>Aid I Recommend for Women Who Have
Experienced Miscarriage:</u>

- Through The Heart: throughtheheart.org
- Caleb Ministries: calebministries.org
- Hannah's Prayer Ministry: hannah.org
- M.E.N.D. Mommies Enduring Neonatal Death: mend.org
- Sufficient Grace Ministries: sufficientgraceministries.com
- Babyloss: babyloss.com
- Miscarriage Support Aukland, Inc.: miscarriagesupport.org.nz
- March of Dimes: marchofdimes.com
  - Parents or other family members who have experienced the loss of a baby between conception and the first month

of life can receive a free March of Dimes bereavement kit by contacting the Fulfillment Center at 1-800-367-6630 or at bkit@marchofdimes.com

- Book: "When God Doesn't Fix It: Lessons You Never Wanted to Learn, Truths You Can't Live Without" by Laura Story
- Book: "Miscarriage: A Shattered Dream" by Sherokee Isle, Linda Hammer Burns
- Book: "Empty Arms: Coping With Miscarriage, Stillbirth and Infant Death" by Sherokee Ilse
- Book: "A Guide For Fathers: When A Baby Dies" by Tim Nelson
- National Suicide Prevention Lifeline: 1-800-273-8255

These are only a few resources, so please also check with local hospitals and mental health centers for pregnancy loss support groups and programs.

Sources

[1] Amos, Tori. "Tori Amos tv show "miscarriage" interview on UK tv 2002." *YouTube*, uploaded by ToriAmosMcCartney, 8 July 2006, https://www.youtube.com/watch?v=N1tr8LLl6qM.

[2] Closer Staff. "EXCLUSIVE: Duck Dynasty's Jase & Missy Robertson Reveal 'We Had a Miscarriage.'" *Closer Weekly Magazine.* 30 April 2014. http://www.closerweekly.com/posts/duck-dynasty-s-jase-missy-robertson-reveal-we-had-a-miscarriage-37748. Accessed 16 October 2016.

[3] Dickens, Charles. *Great Expectations.* New York: Barnes & Noble Books, 2003. Print.

[4] Dion, Celine. "Celine Dion on Her Miscarriage." *YouTube*, uploaded by clipsism, 12 December 2009, https://www.youtube.com/watch?v=Kcf1ZMCh458.

[5] Dion, Celine. "Celine Dion on Oprah 2010." *YouTube*, uploaded by CelineFan, 18 July 2015, https://www.youtube.com/watch?v=AViwkmBw2E4.

[6] Jay Z. ""Glory." Show You How To Do This Pt. 1, Puff-A-Lot Records, 31 January 2012.

[7] Kendrick, Keith. "Lily Allen Talks For First Time About Devastating Stillbirth Of Her First Child." *Huffpost Parents*, Huffpost. 20 May 2015, http://www.huffingtonpost.co.uk/2014/08/14/lily-allen-talks-for-first-time-about-devastating-stillbirth-of-her-first-child_n_7329682.html. Accessed 16 October 2016.

[8] Ravitz, Justin. "Beyoncé Opens Up About Her Miscarriage: 'The Saddest Thing I've Ever Been Through.'" *Weekly US Magazine*, 31 January 2013, http://www.usmagazine.com/celebrity-moms/news/beyonce-opens-up-about-her-miscarriage-the-saddest-thing-ive-ever-been-through-2013311. Accessed 16 October 2016.

[9] Scott, Hillary. "Lady Antebellum Star Hillary Scott on Miscarriage Struggles." *YouTube*, uploaded by Good Morning America, 20 June 2016, https://www.youtube.com/watch?v=bcfGqqQXWRI.

[10] Silverman, Stephen M. "Nicole Kidman Reveals Miscarriage." *People Magazine*, 4 September 2007, http://people.com/celebrity/nicole-kidman-reveals-miscarriage/. Accessed 16 October 2016.

[11] Souter, Erika. "Christie's Heartbreak." *People Magazine*, 31 July 2006, http://people.com/archive/christies-heartbreak-vol-66-no-5/. Accessed 16 October 2016.

[12] Strayed, Cheryl. *Tiny Beautiful Things: Advice on Love and Life from Dear Sugar*. New York: Vintage Books, A Division of Random House, Inc., 2012. Print.

[13] "The Japanese Art of Fixing Broken Pottery With Gold." *Amazing Planet*, 28 May 2014, http://www.amusingplanet.com/2014/05/kintsugi-japanese-art-of-fixing-broken.html.

[14] "This Is Life." *The View*, created by Barbara Walters and Bill Geddie, interview with Lisa Ling, season 14, episode 12.10.10, Lincoln Square Productions (ABC News), 2010.

[15] Williams, Ashley. "I Need to Talk About My Miscarriage." Standard Blog. *Human Development Project*. HPD.Press. 9 September 2016. Web. 16 October 2016.

Printed in the United States
By Bookmasters